Bazooka Proof

BAZOOKA PROOF

Create a Foundation of Fulfillment So Your Happiness Can Thrive

BRIAN N. HIGHFIELD

NEW YORK

LONDON • NASHVILLE • MELBOURNE • VANCOUVER

BAZOOKA PROOF

Create a Foundation of Fulfillment So Your Happiness Can Thrive

Published in New York, New York, by Morgan James Publishing. Morgan James is a trademark of Morgan James, LLC. www.MorganJamesPublishing.com

ISBN 9781642798982 paperback
ISBN 9781642798999 eBook
Library of Congress Control Number: 2019953458

Cover and Interior Design by:
Chris Treccani
www.3dogcreative.net

Morgan James is a proud partner of Habitat for Humanity Peninsula and Greater Williamsburg. Partners in building since 2006.

Get involved today! Visit
MorganJamesPublishing.com/giving-back

DEDICATION

For my son Austin who will understand how to turn hopes and dreams into reality for himself and for others. To my wife Holly who gives balance to my life and unselfishly helps so many people. And for my parents who unknowingly provided a wonderful path to my achievements in life.

TABLE OF CONTENTS

ACKNOWLEDGMENTS

There are countless people who have had an impact on my life in some shape or form. Most of whom unknowingly contributed to shaping my thoughts over the years into what has become principles in this book. Of course, my parents and many siblings were my first inspirations in setting my life's direction. An endless rotation of mentors entered my life to give me advice and teach me new thoughts at different stages.

Although this book has been nothing more than an aspiration of mine for decades, it wasn't until I made the decision to sit down and begin to write it that it took shape, thanks to some help from John Maxwell's "Rule of 5" which helps me complete large tasks by consistently performing activities every day that contribute to my goals .

In my career, I have had many mentors whom I gleaned golden nuggets and pearls of wisdom from, which I hope to pass along to the next generation. My mentors have helped me sort out what is really important in life and what will fade like yesterday's news.

Lastly, I cannot forget the doubters, the naysayers and dream stealers that I have encountered since childhood for they have motivated me more than anything else.

"I owe my enemies a great debt, because they redoubled my energies and drove me in new directions."

–Edward O. Wilson

INTRODUCTION

There was a point in my life when I liked being depressed, and that scared me. When I was little, I had a lot going for me, but I couldn't always see it. There was a time when I searched for everything going wrong in my life, and I always found it. One day, it was about not being tall enough. Another day, it was that I didn't have any money to buy something I wanted. The next day, it was about being rejected by someone I liked, or maybe I couldn't hit the baseball as far as the other kids. Whatever it was, this cycle repeated in my head each week. I would lay down in bed at night and take inventory of all the things going wrong in my life, and it made me cry. But, it was strange because I liked thinking about things that made me sad. I liked being depressed, and that was scary. At some point, I realized that if this pattern continued, it would be very unhealthy and I would find myself in a dark place that I couldn't get out of.

Looking back, there was so much to appreciate. In fact, there were more things to appreciate than to be depressed about. I grew up in the late 1970s and early 1980s when school kids went anywhere without supervision. As long as we came home before the streetlights came on, our parents didn't mind. We rode our bikes without helmets, drank from the garden hose, and left the front doors unlocked. My friends and I played all over the neighborhood and beyond. We rode our bikes until the tread on the tires was bald (even then, we kept going!).

I had a loving family, plenty of siblings, decent clothes, my own room (after my brother moved out) and farmland to play in and explore. There was plenty to be thankful for, but I was stuck thinking about what I didn't have. I was comparing my life to the seemingly wonderful lives my friends had. They had money to buy what they wanted, their families went to Disneyland, they ate at the fancy restaurants, and they had girlfriends and excelled in sports. Or at least, that's how I saw it. It was a perception that my brain bought into, and it contrasted from my reality.

The days of the 1970s and 1980s are long gone. It's a much different world now. Kids need helmets and padding to ride their bikes, front doors are locked, and we have to worry about the internet, cell phones, and other technology ruining our children. But, some things never change, no matter the era. There is always something you can find to be sad about. Likewise, as I learned later, there is always something you can find to be happy about. Whether you are looking for good things or bad things, you will always find what you are looking for.

There was a point in my childhood when I made a decision to change my outlook. If I didn't, I knew I'd be in real trouble. That decision was immediate, but my mindset took much longer to change. Over the course of growing into a young adult and then decades after leaving home for college, I began to develop habits that ultimately put me on a path of mental toughness and confidence. With me, some of my habits now verge on OCD, but in the end, I became one of the happiest people I knew.

I was accepted into the most selective university in the state of Ohio even though I couldn't afford tuition. I knew that I could figure out how to make it work. I worked two part time jobs, took out some very large student loans and borrowed the remaining $3,000 from my grandfather. After graduating with a degree in Engineering, I immediately entered the fast growing field of Information Technology. The fast paced IT industry taught me numerous lessons in business and in human behavior. I quickly rose through the ranks to what was to become one of the largest communications firms in the world. My career was my life until it wasn't. I retired from that company at age 44 with a buyout and went into business for myself.

I coached high school volleyball for many years and that experience led me to my 2nd career as a business owner. I was fortunate in creating two multi-million dollar businesses. One in the area of sports and the other in the area of health and wellness. It's funny to look back and see how everything is connected and each experience was a stepping stone to the next.

Over the past two-and-a-half decades, I've consider myself one of the most positive people you could meet. It's a complete 180 degrees from the little boy crying at night thinking of all the things that made him sad. Was it good fortune and circumstances that made this transformation happen? Maybe in part, but I believe you can create your own luck and change your own circumstances. A new direction is just one decision away. I began to seek out opportunity and prepared myself to seize upon it. I also began to philosophize on the feelings of happiness and their deeper meaning. I also realized that happiness is what I sought, but how do you keep it once you find it?

What makes you happy? Why are some people more positive and prosperous than others? Is it their circumstances or maybe their demographics? Maybe it has to do more with mindset. I've asked myself these questions for most of my adult life. There seems to be an abundance of self-help books, seminars, and research findings that try to help people find their own happiness. In my unprofessional opinion, I think most of them are focusing on characteristics of happy people and psychological factors, but I believe there is something more foundational at play here.

Although I'm an educated person, I'm not a formally educated psychologist, nor do I have any clinical training in psychology or psychiatry. I haven't performed exhaustive research on what does or doesn't make one happy. I am simply someone who considers themselves an extremely positive and happy person. I have felt this way for most of my life now, and I have put a lot of thought into why that is. As a result, I need to share my own conclusions and see if I can connect with anyone who may be pursuing happiness but is feeling exhausted or even frustrated in doing so.

When it comes to creating happiness, I think the current conversations in the self-help world today are misguided for the most part. I want you to focus on something a little bit more concrete than the feeling of happiness and to create something that is much less elusive. One you understand the 5 laws outlined in this book and apply them to your own life, you can give yourself more confidence and mental toughness, and you can be happy more often.

What I've discovered within myself was quite a revelation to me, and I'm convinced that any person can discover the same within themselves. I'm not joking when I say these discoveries are nothing short of superpowers within each one us. Once you realize you have them, you can use them for good or for spiteful purposes. Once you discover them, you can wield great strength over those who have not yet discovered them. More importantly, this knowledge unshackles those who understand and respect its significance. No, this is not a comic book where the superhero learns of their new-found powers. This is your life, and I want to help people like you get the most out of it.

CHAPTER 1

The Elusive Goal of Happiness

"We hold these truths to be self-evident, that all men are created equal, that they are endowed by their Creator with certain unalienable Rights, that among these are Life, Liberty and the pursuit of Happiness."

– UNITED STATES DECLARATION OF INDEPENDENCE

When Thomas Jefferson drafted the Declaration of Independence, he included the statement that the pursuit of happiness is an unalienable right endowed by man's creator. Scholars debate on his inspiration for this notable quote, but scholars agree that he was using the philosophical definition of happiness, which is more about having a prosperous life, than the psychological definition of happiness, which has to do more with a state of mind. In today's society, most refer to happiness as the latter.

Throughout time, happiness has always been a topic of conversation. I often wonder what the Neanderthals did to convey their feelings of content after eating a barbequed mammoth. In more recent times, thousands of self-help books try to teach people about how to feel and stay happy. Numerous studies have been commissioned to determine what makes people happy. Researchers, who are far geekier than me, have even quantified happiness into an equation based on demographics and socioeconomic characteristics. Did you ever want to calculate your happiness? You can by exploring the world of "happiness economics." I'm not joking – it's a real thing.

Again, most people in modern society equate happiness with its psychological definition of the emotional state of well-being. People are seeking something that is often evading them, and they tell themselves stories of how to achieve happiness, such as getting more money, maybe a better job, or possibly meeting their soulmate. People are chasing their tails by consistently saying, "I'll be happy if…" or, "I'll be happy when…". For example, they may say things like,

"I'll be happy if I get a promotion," or, I'll be happy if I can afford that new car," or, "I'll be happy when I meet that special someone." I believe most people know that happiness doesn't come that way, at least not for very long. The obvious problem with this mentality is that the job is never good enough, the car doesn't stay new, and relationships are hard to maintain. The utopian story that we often tell ourselves is not only unrealistic, but it puts ourselves on a hamster wheel that only goes round and round but never really gets us to where we want to go. However, one positive is that it does have the benefit of giving one hope that they can be happy one day, but they will inevitably get stuck on that hamster wheel and the happiness can gets kicked down the road again.

> "When I went to school, they asked me what I wanted to be when I grew up. I wrote down 'happy.' They told me I didn't understand the assignment, and I told them they didn't understand life."
> — **JOHN LENNON**

I had bouts of depression growing up. I wasn't clinically diagnosed. It never got to that point, but I remember lying in bed feeling sad and often crying because of something that I felt was wrong or felt unfair in my life. It could have been that I was too short, too poor, or didn't have the friends that I wanted, or the girl

I liked at school didn't like me back. It could have been any number of things, but what scared me the most was that I liked being depressed. It felt good. I invented things to be sad about, and the fact that I liked it was frightening. It scared me. I sat and began to think about my life and what I actually had going for me. I shouldn't have been depressed at all. I had too many things going right in my life, and there were many activities that I enjoyed. I was grateful that I was in a loving family and that my parents provided what they did for me and my four siblings while working minimum-wage jobs. Fortunately for me, I began a journey to be more grateful and more self-aware and to figure out how to be happy more often. Many of the experiences I had throughout this journey became habits, and over the next thirty years, I began to organize the thoughts that created my current mindset. This resulted in the five laws outlined in this book. These five laws, when applied, can build a solid foundation in which happiness can thrive. Instead of just chasing happiness, I found myself happy more often. Better yet, I became not only resilient to the defeats we experience in everyday life, but I've become bazooka-proof to where my joy is unshakable most times. It truly is a mindset that you can learn and practice over time to build your own solid resolve to feel joy, happiness, and best of all, fulfilled.

Before getting into the laws of fulfillment, let's talk about most people's mindset and how they view happiness. I'm going to generalize here as people vary greatly in their mindsets and views on different states of their being.

I remember being overcome with joy after getting my first car. It was a hand-me-down from one of my sisters. It was a 1984 Ford Escort in a lovely dirt brown color. It was an upgrade from my souped-up moped that my mother bought for me when I was fourteen. Of course, the first thing I did to the car is upgrade the radio from the stock AM/FM to a store-bought deluxe model with a cassette player. I also added speakers to the rear seats so I could turn up the base to my favorite Metallica or Guns N Roses songs to impress the ladies at my high school. It was a "chick magnet," but only in my head. The car lived a short life, as the engine overheated twice, blowing the engine head each time. We sold it for scrap when I was a junior in high school, which left me carpooling with my friends instead of driving my own car with an available front seat that was saved for a possible girlfriend.

My second car was purchased right before graduating college. It was a black Honda Accord with gold wheels. I can tell what you're thinking right now: *He got all the girls with that car.* Well, not exactly, but I was happy with it until a new car model came out. I bought one of those after I graduated college, and it was nice until even newer models came out. I traded my car in for an even newer model. I was happy with that but after driving it for tens of thousands of miles, I wanted something new and different. I saved up and purchased a Porsche Boxster, which I was thrilled with and drove for a few years, but I soon wanted something even better, so I traded it in and bought a Porsche 911 Turbo with all the options. I still own that car today. The desire for a newer, better car was never ending.

If you are my age or older, you probably have a similar story about getting a car and feeling really happy the day you got it, but the newness and excitement wanes and you set your sights on something different that makes you happy again, at least when you first get it. This cycle probably repeated itself as it did with me until you reached the age when you had kids and it didn't matter what car you wanted; you succumbed to the reality of owning a minivan or an SUV to cart the kids and the dog around town while envying the young guys and gals who drove in their fancy red sports cars.

The feeling of often wanting a new car to be happy is an example of the cycle we get in. Thinking, "I'll be happy when I can afford that new car," only gives us that fleeting moment of joy when we get the new car, but that joy erodes fairly quickly, and over the lifetime of owning that car, the joy is only at the beginning and the vast majority of that time, we wish we had something new to feel the joy again. This cycle plays out with other desires in our life, such as our job, our house, and even our relationships, especially if you're lacking one. These are all examples of chasing happiness as a response to an outcome. It's a vicious cycle of "if this happens, then I'll be happy" mindset. Happiness and joy are not sustainable with this mindset. We spend most of our time chasing our tail with only sparse moments of happiness and joy. The gaps in between become a vacuum where other emotions that are less desirable seep in, like anxiety, stress, frustration and even apathy. Chasing happiness is about as nonsensical and unfulfilling as a dog chasing its tail.

By definition, happiness is a psychological emotion. An emotion by definition is a state derived from one's circumstances, mood or relationships, among other things. What do circumstances, moods, and relationships have in common? They are temporary, and they change quite often. Therefore, the emotion of happiness is also temporary. So, why are we pursuing happiness when it is only temporary? Is there something more permanent or at least semi-permanent that we can spend our time and energy on? I will tell you that there most definitely is.

There is something out there that trumps happiness, at least in terms of where you should focus your time in building. There is something that if you create it, it will allow you to experience happiness much more often. If you master it, sadness and discontent will become as rare as Bigfoot sightings.

Happiness is a response to an outcome. We tell ourselves, if this happens, then I'll be happy. But, for how long? This cause-and-effect relationship in our head is a vicious cycle. As soon as we achieve the "if," we raise the bar to a whole new level and we reset our mindset to be "unhappy" until we achieve the next goal. This cycle has a name, and it is called the "hedonic treadmill." If you've been on a treadmill, you notice that you get tired and sweaty but your body remains in the same place when you finish as when you started. In our topic of happiness, your level of happiness (or unhappiness) gets reset to the same place as when you started, before achieving your goal, even after you achieve it. It sounds crazy, I know. It is crazy! How can we achieve a steady and more constant level of happiness in our lives when our brain keeps moving the goal posts? What I am proposing here is that we exchange our pursuit of happiness for a foundation of fulfillment. Let's build a platform that has longevity and is more of a constant than the temporary, cyclic nature of happiness and joy. You see, fulfillment is an asset more than it is a feeling or emotion. Once it is built correctly, your foundation of fulfillment is an asset that cannot be taken away from you.

This book will help you recognize and build an asset that is more important than the temporary emotion of happiness or joy. One benefit of this asset is that you will find yourself happy more often. It will help you springboard your emotions into a positive mindset to where happiness and joy will be discovered.

What makes people happy?

Think of a time when you were most happy. If you are like most people, you're thinking of an event, such as a wedding, buying a new car, getting a job, a first kiss, or possibly a dream vacation. As that event shifts from the present and into the past, the joy you felt slips from the present and becomes a memory. Our lives go back to the normal median of the spectrum. What really makes us happy? Is it the occasion? We are certainly happier at celebrations than we are at our job. Is it our location? We are happier at an exotic vacation than inside our own home. Is it the people we surround ourselves with? We are usually more happy being around our friends than strangers. There has been a lot of research and studies conducted on determining the happiest cities in America or even the happiest places in the world. After reading articles on such topics, you may want to move to Boulder, Colorado, which topped the list of happiest cities in America in a 2017 study. The book *The Blue Zones of Happiness* by Dan Buettner has the complete list of cities in America and places abroad that find the world's happiest people, and it examines why these people are so happy. If you watch any news reports about studies like the ones outlined in the book, unless you already live in the happiest city, you might think that you have to move to one of these places in order to be happy. So, pack up your clothes, your pets, and that spoon collection and let's load the U-Haul trailer and get moving. Happiness awaits! You wouldn't know it from the press coverage but the message from this book is not that you have to move to one of these places to be happy; it is about applying the characteristics of these locations to your life, no matter where you live. So, hold off on buying that plane ticket to Denmark, which topped the list of the happiest places on earth.

So, what are those characteristics? What do the blue zones of happiness all have in common? I believe all of them have built a foundation of fulfillment that provides a springboard for a positive mindset. When this happens, happiness can thrive. This book will discuss the applied laws that are intrinsic to your happiness and wellbeing.

The Artist and the Businessman

On a summer weekend, a foreign businessman was vacationing in Mexico. He took a walk through the town center and happened upon an art festival in the middle of the town square.

As he strolled through the exhibits admiring the different styles and creativity of each artist, he saw there was a crowd of people gathered around one particular exhibit. There was quite a commotion, as tourists and even locals were clamoring over and buying the paintings in and around the exhibit.

The businessman moved closer and watched in amazement as the buyers weren't even haggling over the price. They were simply grabbing the art and handing over the money as fast as they could. He noticed a small man with a beard and mustache collecting the money and presumed he was also the creator of the highly desired pieces of art. The businessman watched in amazement as the money surged from the customers to the artist in a seemingly never-ending flow.

After about twenty or so minutes, almost all the works of art were sold. Only a few small pieces remained under the white tent of the artist. The artist began to pack up his things as he had successfully sold most of his work. The businessman, still in awe of the flood of transactions that he just witnessed, saw an opportunity and approached the artist to have a conversation.

"Hi there!" said the businessman as he approached the artist who was still packing up his things. "Do you speak English?" the businessman asked.

"Yes," said the artist with a slight accent.

The businessman walked up to the artist and introduced himself. The artist stopped what he was doing and the businessman, excited with thoughts racing through his head, began to ask the artist questions.

"I noticed you are almost sold out, and it's still early in the day. Is this normal for you?"

"Yes," replied the artist. "My art brings many of the tourists and even some of the locals much joy. They love my style, and it seems to make them happy."

"Wow!" said the businessman. "Is this all you do? I mean, what else do you do?"

The artist smiled and answered the question. "Oh, well, every day, I like to fish in the morning, create art during the day, play with my children after school, eat dinner with my wife and kids, and drink, sing and dance with my wife and friends at night."

The businessman, confused by the response, said, "No, I meant, is the sale of your art your only income?"

"Yes," replied the artist. "I create my art during the week and sell it one day each weekend."

The businessman, with so many business ideas racing through his head, could hardly contain himself.

"But, your artwork is in such high demand. We could get you in multiple galleries across the world. We can create a shipping infrastructure for your artwork and create a marketing strategy and a website. You would have to spend many hours each week painting and creating art for several years, but you could make a lot of money, be rich and retire!"

The businessman paused to catch his breath and to see how the artist would react to his ideas.

The artist looked inquisitively at the businessman and asked, "Retire? What would I do when I retire?"

The businessman, intrigued by the question, replied, "Well, whatever you want. Whatever makes you happy."

"You know what I would do?" the artist asked.

The businessman shook his head.

"Every day, I would fish in the morning, create art during the day, play with my children after school, eat dinner with my wife and kids, and drink, sing and dance with my wife and friends at night."

The artist then put on his hat, gathered his things and said farewell to the businessman. As the artist walked away towards home, the businessman stood still and scratched his chin with a puzzled look on his face.

Money and Happiness

"Money is numbers, and numbers never end. If it takes money to be happy, your search for happiness will never end."

– Bob Marley

As everyone says, money can't buy happiness, but everyone still wants to prove it for themselves. Now, money is required to live. It ranks right up there with oxygen. We use money as a means to trade for things that we need and also for things we want but don't need. Money does bring options and can afford us a better quality of life, which can affect our happiness, but we also have the power to overcome that, just as the artist did in the story. He made just enough each week to live the life he wanted. He lives a lifestyle that makes him happy and wasn't caught up in the businessman's mindset that more money will bring more happiness.

Don't get me wrong. I would rather be sad inside a Ferrari than on top of a bicycle. And I do believe that there is opportunity all around us, and if more financial resources can afford a better quality of life for you and your family, you need to go for it. Just don't lose sight that time is more valuable than money, so invest your time wisely. If you get stuck on that hamster wheel, and you aren't getting ahead, it's hard to get off. There will always be ways to get more money, but we can never buy more time on this earth. Make sure you are spending your time on what matters. At some point in life, it doesn't matter where the commas and decimal points are in your bank account's balance. It's pointless to be the richest man in the cemetery.

Build a foundation of fulfillment

The following chapters will define an asset you can build for yourself so your happiness can thrive. The asset is a foundation of sorts. It is a solid structure that is immovable. It will become your shield from all that life can throw at you. With this shield, you are protected from any assault on your wellbeing. With practice, you can develop habits that fortify your shield, and your life will be healthier, happier, and much more fulfilled. You can become bazooka-proof.

CHAPTER 2

Fulfillment Is the Foundation

Happiness and the Old Alley Cat

(A version of this fable has been told many times in books and articles and is attributed to Dr. Wayne Dyer)

An old alley cat was wandering by the street as a young kitten was chasing his tail. The old cat stopped and asked the kitten, "Young kitten, why are you chasing your tail?"

The kitten didn't stop chasing his tail and tried to respond while breathing heavily. "I heard that happiness is located in your tail," the kitten huffed. "If I catch my tail, I believe I will have eternal happiness." The kitten continued to go round and round, feverishly trying to catch his tail.

"Ah, I see," chuckled the old alley cat. "Well, I've been walking these streets for many years, and I believe you are right. Happiness is inside our tails."

The kitten, out of breath, stopped chasing his tail for a moment to rest. While panting heavily, the kitten said to the old alley cat, "Really? Did you catch your tail and get eternal happiness?"

The old alley cat sat on his hind legs, looked up at the sky and said, "No young one, I never caught it."

Puzzled, the young kitten looked at the alley cat and asked, "Well, what happened then?"

The old alley cat looked down at the kitten with a grin. He stood up and started to walk away with his tail facing back towards the kitten. He then turned his head towards the young one and before walking away, he said, "I found that if I go about my day, and live the way I want to, my tail follows me everywhere I go."

* * *

Why is it that once you achieve a certain goal in your life, like buying that new car, having the night of your life with a significant other, or getting that promotion at work, the euphoria seems so short-lived? The happiness you feel begins to fade, and then your new situation becomes your new normal. As normalcy sets in, the buzz you were feeling wears off. The happiness and joy only last hours or days, and then your mind goes through a kind of reset. Your brain wants something new in order to feel happy again. Are we programmed to be miserable? Is that why our euphoria is just a fleeting moment? I really don't think our lives are supposed to be mundane or that we are supposed to be miserable for most of our existence. We want to experience happiness as much as possible. That's why we chase it so much, just like the kitten chasing his tail in the story. Unfortunately, we always lose in the long run. Our brain craves variety and learning, which contributes to our brain's reset on what makes us happy. Do you think we might be wrong to focus on what brings us happiness to feel happy? I believe our focus should be on something else. How about focusing on being fulfilled?

If we shouldn't focus on what makes us happy in the short-term, then what can we focus on to make us happy long-term? The answer is fulfillment. In order to experience happiness as much as possible, we must first build fulfillment in our minds and hearts. But wait—it gets better. I also believe this foundation of fulfillment not only allows one to be happier more often, but it will allow a person to be more powerful in their life, their thoughts, their relationships and in conquering their goals. The possibilities are endless! This power is a form of resilience and mental toughness. When you understand its full potential, it can make you not only resilient, not only bulletproof, but bazooka-proof.

There is a difference in being resilient and bazooka-proof. It's kind of like the difference between water-resistant and waterproof. Resilience is our ability to recover or bounce back from a setback or disappointment. For example, something didn't go your way or as expected, and that made you unhappy. Being bulletproof is not getting knocked down in the first place. The unfortunate event bounces off you like bullets off Superman. Fulfillment becomes a foundation or a baseline in which we can rely, no matter the circumstances. It's a line in the sand that things cannot cross. When this foundation is fortified, misfortune, calamity, and hopelessness slip off you like a Teflon pan.

Before we get to in-depth on what fulfillment can do for someone, let's talk about what fulfillment actually means. For the purposes of this book, we will define fulfillment as a meaningful realization of your endowments, both mental and physical. It is the ability to appreciate what you possess, including current skills and potential abilities. It includes other things like meaningful relationships, physical possessions, and other accomplishments or talents that add value to you as a person.

What's the difference between happiness and fulfillment? For the purpose of this book, we are going with definitions of these two words that differ in many ways.

Happiness is a temporary emotion where fulfillment is a more permanent mindset that cannot be taken from you. Fulfillment is an asset that you can possess where happiness is an elusive state of mind most of the time. Happiness and joy can be more easily taken away where fulfillment is a foundation where happiness and joy can be built upon. Fulfillment is constant stability and not a response to an outcome.

Your fulfillment is a collective of your abilities and talents, relationships that you value, physical possessions and other things that you give value to. The collection of these valued assets sets the foundation on your emotional response to life's current circumstances. Just the fact that you are alive and breathing gives you a competency over those who are not. Your health is an asset even if you are in poor health (because you're not dead). That may sound overly simple but I'm making a point here. If you have at least one friend or family member that you enjoy spending time with, that is an asset. If you have a roof over your head and can find food when you are hungry, that is an asset. If you have a skill, whether it is knowledge, being computer-savvy, raising children, knowing how to do brain surgery or how to swing a hammer, it is an asset. All these, combined with all your other talents, abilities, relationships, possessions and other things that are of value, creates a foundation that is stable and constant. Without vast effort, they cannot be taken away, and they are there to be appreciated. They make up the foundation that is fulfillment. From this foundation stems feelings such as gratitude, confidence, mental toughness, and especially happiness.

Remember the story of the three little pigs? Three pigs left home to be on their own. One built a house out of straw, one built a house out of twigs and the third built a house out of bricks. When the big bad wolf came calling, the houses out of straw and twigs blew over easily, sending the two pigs running to join their brother in the brick house. The brick house could not be blown over by the big bad wolf, and that made the pigs happy. Most people live in houses made of straw and twigs, at least mentally and emotionally. When you build your foundation of fulfillment, it's like living in a brick house that cannot be blown over by the big bad circumstances of our lives.

When we recognize the feeling of being fulfilled, we don't sweat the big stuff, let alone the small stuff. When we remember what we have, what we don't have becomes less important. It also gives us confidence in what we can do and how we approach each day. When you know you have something that can't be taken away from you, it permits a more positive perspective. Fulfillment is the key to a long-term life with abundant joy. Look at building fulfillment as an investment strategy. You are building an asset that is going to pay off in happiness more often.

As I grew from being a little kid who was often depressed about the things I didn't have, I made some choices about myself that turned into non-negotiable traits. It scared me that I liked being depressed, so I decided to change my mindset. The first thing I recognized was that I had the ability to make that decision. I chose to create a mindset with a more positive outlook. Over the next thirty years, I began to make some discoveries about human behavior that allowed me to analyze and formulate the five laws outlined in this book. I then began to identify habits that I had developed from my new-found mindset. The last chapter in this book offers an action plan for anyone to use to develop their mindset and to build their own foundation of fulfillment.

CHAPTER 3

Law of Self-Actualization

"No one can make you feel inferior
without your consent."

– ELEANOR ROOSEVELT

As we begin to outline the five laws of fulfillment, we must begin with a simple law, but it is also the most important one to understand. Don't assume the simplicity of how it sounds makes you skim through the details. If you can master this law, your mindset will be ahead of 90% of the people out there. My aim here is to make you self-aware of a very important trait that lies within us all but goes unused and unnoticed by most people on the planet. It is truly a superpower.

Law of Fulfillment #1:
The Law of Self-Actualization

The law of self-actualization says that you and only you get to decide how you feel at any moment in time. No one has the power to make you feel a way that you do not choose. If you don't make a choice on how you feel, someone else will.

This may seem obvious to some and may sound simple at first, but please take a moment to appreciate the power that this gives an individual. We have the power to choose what we feel at any moment in time. That is the good news! The bad news is, if you do not make that choice, someone else will. Making a conscious choice takes practice. You need to build your mindset so you make good choices for the best way to feel. You need to be the gatekeeper for your thoughts because thoughts lead to ideas, ideas lead to more thoughts, and then those thoughts lead you to decisions. If you're not minding the gate, someone else can choose your thoughts and make those decisions for you.

This is more about being self-aware. I didn't call this law the law of self-awareness because it's more complicated and more powerful than just being self-aware. I chose the term *self-actualization* from Maslow's hierarchy of needs. Self-actualization is the top tier of Abraham Maslow's theory of human motivation, but it was first introduced by a theorist named Kurt Goldstein for the motive to realize one's full potential. Maslow defined self-actualization to be "the desire for self-fulfillment" and "to become everything that one is capable of becoming." We will talk about strategies to do just that in a later chapter, but for now, absorb and appreciate the fact that we have the power to choose our thoughts and feelings. But beware: if you don't make the choice, someone else will. If that's the case, you are just giving your power away.

One Day in High School

Katy and Tori live across town from each other but go to the same high school. On a Monday morning at 6:45am, the alarm clocks in each of their rooms go off. The girls reluctantly get out of bed and begin to get ready for school. Tori, dreading it's Monday, begins to think about how long the week is going to be and feels depressed that the school year isn't going to end for another two months. Katy, on the other hand, feels a little more upbeat and curious about what the week will have in store for her. She's anxiously anticipating the summer break in two months.

Upon arriving at school, Tori walks in the entrance where a group of girls who are called the Goth Dolls are loitering about, ready to make fun of whomever walks through the doors. The Goth Dolls wear all black, dye their hair different colors, and accessorize their clothes with metal and lace. Their job, as they see it, is to point out the misfortunes of others.

"Get your hair done at Best Cuts?" the one Goth Doll asks Tori as the other Dolls chuckle. Tori looks down at her shoes and quickens her pace. She runs her fingers through the ends of her hair, wondering if it looks that bad. Her week is starting off just as she expected: bad.

Soon after, Katy walks in through the same entrance. The Goth Dolls are ready to pounce.

"When did Walmart start giving haircuts?" the same Goth Doll blurts at Katy as the rest of the Dolls chuckle at the dig similar to Tori's.

Katy smiles at the Dolls as she continues on her way to her locker. For a moment, Katy thinks about what the future may hold for the Dolls. Fast-food, maybe? She feels a little guilty for having an unkind thought but for only a second. She focuses on getting her books for first period from her locker.

Tori and Katy's favorite class is English. They have the same teacher, who they love, but they are in different periods of that class. Tori has English during 3rd period and Katy has it 5th period.

During 3rd period, Tori is interested in the lesson that day. They are discussing the book *The Great Gatsby*. The teacher, whom she loves, asks a question and Tori is eager to answer. Before the teacher can even call on Tori after raising her hand, Tori blurts out her answer in a loud confident voice.

"No," the teacher says with a confused look. "That's incorrect. Who has an answer that makes sense?"

The classroom fills with subtle laughter and snickering as Tori shrinks in her chair, feeling mortified. She had been so excited to answer that she blurted out what first came to mind instead of thinking about it more. Tori's day is getting worse.

In 5th period English, Katy has a similar experience when she blurts out an answer that is also incorrect. The teacher puts her hand over her face, looks down and shakes her head in dismay. The room, once again, fills with some light laughter and giggling. Katy thinks for a second, and smiles. She knows her answer made no sense. She laughs along with her classmates as she realizes her mistake.

Neither Tori nor Katy know it, but they have a crush on the same boy, Devin. All three take part in Driver's Education class. Tori and Katy are both looking forward to the class, mostly because Devin will be there.

After the school day ends, they both head to Driver's Education. They both arrive early, take their seats and begin to look around anxiously for Devin to walk in, hoping he will sit down next to them. It is looking like Devin isn't going to show, but suddenly, his voice can be heard from the hallway. Both girls spin around to see his arrival into the classroom.

As he enters the doorway, both Katy and Tori are surprised as he has his arm around Jennifer Stinkler. Yes, that is her real name. Jennifer is an awkward and quiet girl who is known as the captain of the Trivia team. She wears braces, has specs of acne on both cheeks, and often wears mom jeans. Jennifer is definitely not someone who should be attracting a guy like Devin. Before entering the classroom, Devin gives Jennifer a big smooch on the lips as the couple slowly let go of each other so Devin can get to class. Katy and Tori witness the whole thing with their mouths largely agape.

As Devin walks in and sits down with his eyes slightly glazed over with young love, Tori and Katy slowly turn their heads back around toward the front of the room.

Tori's head is filled with vexing anger and rage. Her anger and confusion about what she just witnessed consumes her thoughts for the entire class. "How can Devin even like her?" she thinks. Her day and maybe even her week is officially ruined.

Katy, after witnessing the very public display of affection between Devin and Jennifer, is surprised as well. Katy would have never guessed that Devin would be even remotely interested in a girl like Jennifer. She chuckles to herself as she pictures the two playing trivia together. She appreciates the humor in the unlikely couple. Katy smiles and shakes her head as she quickly erases the vision of the two lovebirds from her head. Katy is then able to focus on the day's lesson about how to merge into traffic.

After getting home from school, Katy and Tori are coincidentally surprised by each of their parents: they are going to dinner as a family. Both girls are looking forward to the escape from the normalcy of a Monday and to have a fun meal. They are both starving after their day at school. Both Katy's family and Tori's family end up at the same restaurant, although they don't notice each other in the large dining area for their entire meal.

They even order the same entrée. As the entrées come out, both are disappointed because the food is a little cold. After a few bites, their respective waiters sense something is wrong and inquire with the girls. The waiters apologize, replace their meals with hot ones and add a desert for the table at no charge for their inconvenience.

While Katy is thrilled about a free dessert, Tori feels jilted as now her family, who are all but finished with their meals, must watch her chow on her meal with judging eyes. Katy has fun with it, talking about how good the food tastes and discusses which dessert they should choose. Tori, on the other hand, feels anxiety overeating the dessert. It is mostly empty calories, she thinks to herself. "A moment on the lips, a lifetime on the hips," she murmurs to herself.

After dinner, both families, not having seen each other, head home to their neighborhood in their respective cars. On the drive home, both Katy and Tori stare at the sunset but with opposing thoughts. Tori is glad that the "worst" day is over, but she is already fearing tomorrow and what the rest of the week may bring. Katy, conversely, is looking at the sunset with awe and gratitude. "The sunset is beautiful," she thinks. The day isn't perfect and didn't go quite as expected, but Katy was already looking forward to Tuesday and the week ahead and the adventures each day may bring.

* * *

In the story, our two characters shared almost the exact same experiences throughout their day. While the experiences were the same, their reaction to them couldn't differ more. While Katy was eager to start her week, Tori was depressed that it was Monday. While Tori felt like a target from the bullying Goth Dolls, Katy was composed and confident. While Katy laughed at her mistake in English class, Tori felt ridiculed by her classmates. When Tori stewed in her disgust of Devin's taste in girls, Katy shook her head and moved on. As Tori felt self-conscious and judged at dinner, Katy made the best of it. Even with a beautiful sunset on the horizon, Tori felt sad as it was only Monday while Katy felt grateful and anxious as it was only Monday.

"The greatest weapon against stress is our ability to choose one thought over another."

– WILLIAM JAMES, AMERICAN PHILOSOPHER

Why the different views for the exact same experience? Is it their mindset? Is it their attitude? Is it their level of maturity? You can make a case for any of those, but what it really boils down to is choice. We not only have control over what we are thinking, we also have control over what we are feeling. If we aren't the ones making those choices for ourselves, then who is? The answer is nobody, unless we let them. Not one individual or even a group of people have the power to force us to think certain thoughts or feel any particular way. Someone might try to influence our thoughts and feelings, but we are the final decision maker on what we think or feel at any moment in time.

Let's focus on the fact that you get to choose how you feel and react to any given situation. The next time you feel angry, upset, or sad, take a deep breath and ponder the fact that the feeling you are experiencing at that moment is a choice you make.

This is easier said than done as we get caught up in the moment and emotions seem to take control of our thoughts and we create a story in our head, that is mostly fiction, about how we've been wronged and the situation is an attack on us personally or that someone is trying to get away with something they shouldn't. In reality, we just don't understand the situation in its entirety or what another person wants to accomplish. What they seek to accomplish is usually not for the purposes of making you upset; most often, it's simply a situation of miscommunication or uneven expectations.

I travel a lot, and almost every time I'm in the airport, I see someone arguing with a TSA agent about bringing a bottle of water or some other liquid through the security checkpoint.

This is an example of uneven expectations and miscommunication. The traveler thinks it's perfectly reasonable to bring a harmless bottle of drinking water into the airport. But, they have never heard the rule that you cannot, or more importantly, they don't understand the reason behind the rule. The TSA officer knows that liquid explosives are a real threat and can be disguised as bottles of liquid. The traveler, not knowing or understanding these rules and the reasons behind them, gets upset when they are told to throw it away or to drink it before going through security. This just adds to an already stressful situation. Often times, I hear the TSA agent tell them they cannot bring it in but they often don't tell them why. I think the why part is important so the traveler can understand and reset their expectations so their attitude changes from "I can't believe I can't take this into the airport!" to "Oh, that makes sense" and "I'll know better for next time." The point here is that when we try to understand the situation we are in a little more, we can make better choices regarding if we should feel outraged or be more appreciative. In this case, I can appreciate the TSA agent enforcing a rule that could have life-or-death consequences.

We set ourselves up for disappointment when we lack knowledge or have misguided expectations, as in the case of the inexperienced traveler and the TSA agent. Letting yourself get mad or even furious is your sign that you may be missing a key piece of knowledge and setting your expectations on the unrealistic side of the spectrum.

I coached youth sports for many years, and in this arena, there are countless examples of parents having unrealistic expectations on top of lacking knowledge behind coaching decisions. If you have ever been a coach or around youth sports, you know what I'm talking about. More often than not, a parent feels their child is the "best" player on the team and deserves to be treated as such by getting the most playing time and getting a starting position. From my twenty-plus years of coaching experience, I have an expert perspective on players and their abilities and the team's strategy. The parents often have limited knowledge other than watching their child play through a myopic lens with an abundance of love and care for their child and their well-being. This lens often distorts reality and sets an expectation in their mind that is reinforced by their passion for their child's rearing. Don't get me wrong, their passion as a parent is commendable and their heart is in the right place. But, this can pose a problem by creating a bias that is compounded by their lack of knowledge and understanding of the sport itself and/ or the responsibility of the coach to consider everyone's needs. The end result is a lack of information and unrealistic expectations that differ from the coach; this ultimately comes to a head when those expectations are not met. Emotions take over and anger, slightness, and even outrage push understanding, content and appreciation to the side when the child doesn't receive all the accolades the parent envisioned from the start.

I had a dad upset that his daughter wasn't getting the playing time or starting position that he felt she deserved. His basis was that she was the best player on her school team. We were coaching a club team, which was made up from players from multiple schools who were often the best players from their respective school teams. His expectation was that she would receive the same treatment as she did in high school when the reality was the bar had been raised to a higher standard on a more competitive team.

Another parent was upset about his kid's playing time for a different reason. The sport was volleyball but the dad measured playing time in minutes on the court, which is what you do in basketball. That was the sport he was knowledgeable about. He was new to volleyball, so we had to reset his expectations and educate him on how the game itself determined playing time. We likened the sport to football, which was another sport he was familiar with. We equated his daughter's volleyball offensive position to a quarterback, which is only on the field during offense and is on the bench during defense. The dad then got it and the anger subsided. We were successful in level-setting everyone's expectations.

In situations like these, managing your own expectations and arming yourself with information are within your full control. Deciding to appreciate that your child has a team to play on and a coach who's willing to take the time to give to the team will save yourself a lot of heartache down the road. Understanding that the coach has many players' interests to lookout for should trump anyone's self-interest.

As a coach, we often attempt to head off these issues by communicating up front the philosophies, strategies, and evaluation criteria so that expectations are properly set ahead of time. It was always the parents who didn't come to the pre-season meetings who were tough to deal with. They were the ones whose expectations remained out of balance with our own and were, therefore, different than reality.

These examples in youth sports should give you some insight into the daily decisions we all face, many of which are subliminal in nature, because emotions can cause us to jump to conclusions. Before we "decide" to be angry, fearful, sad or disgusted, let's take a quick assessment of any information we are lacking and also if our expectations are incorrectly set as a result. Ask yourself, is it possible that I'm missing something? Then, decide what you can ask to create clarity and understanding in your situation.

Have you ever made an assumption that turned out to be incorrect? Sometimes, we forget that we assumed. Over a short period of time, our assumption of "it's probably true" turned into "it's "definitely true," and now our expectation is set to a misguided setting. We just set ourselves up for disappointment if it's not true after all. You can witness an example of this on a daily basis by going to a store or restaurant and watching someone trying to use an expired coupon. They made the assumption that the clerk or cashier would overlook that fact and honor the coupon anyway. Some stores will, but some establishments won't. The assumption is forgotten, and disappointment and anger sets in when they didn't get the discount.

To set proper expectations, we need to remind ourselves that there is a level of uncertainty in unfamiliar situations. When we experience new things, we should go in with reasonable but loose expectations to give ourselves and others some wiggle room to work things out emotionally in our head. Some call this "going with the flow." This approach allows our expectations to rebalance themselves so that we are less likely to be disappointed in the end.

Your Mantra

Repeat after me: "I am the only decision maker in how I feel at any given time. I refuse to let anyone make that decision for me, as they do not have that power over me. I will give others the benefit of the doubt as their intentions are not to offend or disappoint me. I will set my expectations properly and reset them as I learn and understand more about the world around me."

CHAPTER 4

Law of Appreciation

"Enjoy the little things in life, for one day, you may look
back and realize they were the big things."

- AUTHOR UNKNOWN

What can a puppy teach a grown man?

David and his wife Gloria decided to get a puppy. Their current dog was Gloria's before they got married. The dog was a small, female, chocolate lab named Mocha. Mocha was a great dog. She was well behaved and loved

Our puppy, Luna

walks and chasing balls. She responded to the owner's commands and was friendly to others. As she got older, David and Gloria wanted a dog as well behaved and with the same temperament as Mocha. They decided to get another lab, but what color?

They thought about yellow, black, and even chocolate like Mocha. But now, there were even more exotic choices such as red fox labs, charcoal labs, and silver labs. After some research into different breeders, they decided on a silver lab puppy. Demand for silver labs was high, so many of the litters were already spoken for. David and Gloria wanted another female like Mocha, and their disappointment mounted as every breeder said the same thing: "No puppies are available. You'll have to wait until the next litter or the one after that." Resorting to this reality, David and Gloria put their name on the waiting list with a well-respected breeder.

Then one day, a surprise! The breeder called Gloria to tell her some news.

"That's wonderful!" Gloria said on the phone as David was overhearing the conversation. "Yes! We are definitely interested, and we will take her!"

After being on the phone for a few minutes, Gloria hung up and turned to David and shared the good news. "The breeder just called, and they have another female silver lab! The litter was just born and they had one more pup than they expected."

"That's wonderful!" David excitedly replied. "It's a female, right?"

"Yes! They have one more female pup than expected, but we get last pick of the females in the litter if we want a puppy."

David and Gloria were elated that they would be getting a puppy sooner rather than later, and they couldn't wait to pick her from the litter and take her home.

There were nine pups in the litter. After everyone else picked their puppy, there was one left waiting for David and Gloria to come pick up and take home. It was the unexpected female who was also the runt of the litter. Although David and Gloria didn't get to pick, they were grateful they didn't have to select between two or more pups and were glad to take the last remaining puppy home.

Gloria and David decided to name her Luna. Gloria had already ordered a custom puppy collar with Luna's name embroidered onto the pink and powder blue collar. They picked Luna up from the breeder and put her new collar on. Luna slept the entire two-hour trip home.

Mocha didn't know what to think about Luna. When Luna woke up, she was a feisty little puppy who wasn't scared of the big chocolate lab. Luna wanted to play with Mocha, but Mocha was a little hesitant. But only at first.

As the initial small-puppy days passed by, Mocha and Luna began playing in the yard, although, if Mocha could talk, she would probably tell you that she was more annoyed by Luna and her antics than playful. Nevertheless, both dogs got along, learned to eat from separate dog bowls and took naps together several times a day.

When Gloria was home, she would often lounge on the sectional sofa and Luna would climb up and curl up in a ball on Gloria's stomach. Gloria called Luna her little cuddlebug because she always seemed to want to cuddle with her.

Now David, on the other hand, hadn't taken care of a puppy since he was a little boy and he'd forgotten or never really experienced the frustrations involved with house training and caring for a puppy. After finding chewed-up shoes, rugs, and other destroyed household items that were anything but her chew toys, the frustration and annoyance started to build. Stained carpet and strange smells only added to David's exasperation.

Sharp puppy teeth left scratches and puncture marks in David's hands. House breaking was a challenge as Luna couldn't go up and down stairs to get to the yard, so messes in the house and on the deck were frequent problems for David and Gloria. What really made David's blood boil was when Luna dug up the yard. David loved keeping his yard manicured and looking nice. Torn up turf and piles of dirt were scattered across the yard. Then, to add to the annoyance, dirt and mud was tracked into the house and Luna's paws would always need to be washed.

In between the frustrations, there were happy times too. Luna was a bundle of energy and loved to play. She learned to fetch and run around the yard, and of course, pester Mocha. Mocha wouldn't admit it, but she enjoyed having a playmate around and loved having a companion. Gloria loved having her little cuddlebug every evening on the couch.

At about four months of age, David and Gloria began to worry. Luna was showing signs of concern such as bleeding gums, bad breath, constipation, and increased thirst. David and Gloria weren't overly concerned and thought it might be a growing phase or from bad dog food, but Gloria was concerned enough to take her to the vet since she needed her shots anyway. The vet didn't express too much concern but took blood samples for analysis.

When the vet called back a couple days later, it wasn't good news. Gloria began to tear up and breathe heavily as the vet told her that the blood tests revealed a problem with Luna's kidneys. David walked in as

Gloria was getting the news. Gloria put the call on speakerphone and David's knees felt week as he sank to the floor as the vet explained that the prognosis was not good but they would need a specialist to evaluate Luna's condition and recommend a course of treatment.

David and Gloria held on to hope as they quickly scheduled an appointment with a specialist to take place a few days later.

One the day of the appointment, a vet assistant picked up Luna from the waiting room and took her back to see the specialist. After about 20 minutes of testing from the specialist, the assistant came to get David and Gloria from the waiting room.

"He's ready to talk to you," she said.

David and Gloria walked into the examination room to meet the specialist. Luna was happy to see her owners and displayed a shaven belly from where the ultrasound had been performed.

After introducing himself and explaining the tests he had done on Luna, the specialist did not have good news.

"I'm afraid her kidneys are undersized and cannot keep up with her growth. This dog should be twice the size she is now."

"What's her prognosis?" David asked.

The specialist paused and said, "I don't expect this dog to be alive for more than a year."

A sinking feeling went through David and Gloria as the hope they had gathered leading up to the appointment started to diminish. The assistant wiped away a tear as she continued to play with Luna in the examination room.

"What can we do?" Gloria asked.

The specialist first said that most dogs in this condition are euthanized. Not because they were in a lot of pain but because it would take a lot of resources to keep them alive. Both Gloria and David immediately said that euthanization was not option at this point. He then prescribed a special diet and the need to get her system flushed intravenously a few times a week to remove toxic buildup in her blood.

After taking Luna home, David and Gloria were still hopeful. They researched kidney disease in dogs and even researched kidney transplants for dogs, which was a new treatment in veterinary science. They gave Luna her special dog food diet and took her in twice a week to the vet to have her system flushed.

After about two weeks, Luna's condition worsened. She acted constipated, would not lie down at night and stood constantly while trying to maintain her balance.

One night was so bad that David and Gloria took her to the emergency vet clinic. They examined Luna and began a continuous intravenous line to flush her system of the toxic buildup in her blood. After keeping her overnight, Gloria and David returned the next day to meet with the vet. She said that Luna would need constant flushing of her system and that they would have another specialist examine Luna closer and determine a course of action. Luna would need to stay in the animal hospital for the foreseeable future. In the meantime, David and Gloria asked about the possibility of a transplant. The veterinarian said that progress had been made in that science for dogs but it was costly and David and Gloria would have to find their own donor dog.

"What!?" said Gloria.

The veterinarian explained. "Yes. Preferably the donor dog would come from the same litter or at least share a parent."

"Who would offer up their dog to donate one of their kidneys?" thought David and Gloria.

After getting home that day, Gloria immediately logged into Facebook and posted Luna's situation, looking for a donor kidney. Many people responded with their thoughts and prayers but chances of finding a donor were slim. No takers yet.

David and Gloria visited Luna a few times a day. Luna was happy to see them when they visited. She seemed like her old self but the veterinarian would only allow the visit to be an hour long before Luna would need to be hooked back up to the IV.

After a new specialist thoroughly examined Luna, David and Gloria sat with the veterinarian to learn more about Luna's condition. Once again, the news was not what David and Gloria had hoped.

"It's not just kidney disease. Luna's kidneys have not developed at all," said the specialist. "I do not expect her to survive more than two months."

After hearing this, the heavy hearts of David and Gloria sank even lower.

The veterinarian recommended a course of treatment in the hope that they could find a donor although she stated that a kidney transplant would be incredibly expensive and risky. But in the meantime, the veterinarian thought Luna's health could be maintained temporarily with the IV treatments. The vet did not recommend euthanization, as she thought Luna's condition was not at a point where she was suffering.

Concerned for Luna's quality of life in the hospital, being hooked up to an IV 24 hours a day, David asked about taking Luna home. The vet said it was up to them, but Luna would need to be brought back for IV treatments every day.

"I just think she needs the chance to be a dog again and to be home," said David.

Gloria agreed and Luna was taken home the next day. It was a warm sunny day, and Luna was happy to be home. She eagerly went around the house sniffing everything as if she was there for the first time. She played with her big sister, Mocha, the chocolate lab. Luna played in the backyard and dug up David's yard and plants.

As David watched her dig up his precious landscaping and get all dirty and muddy, he just smiled and laughed. She was a puppy again!

David realized right there and then that he didn't have to be angry and frustrated by the antics of a puppy doing what they do best. Chewing up shoes, digging in the yard or going potty on the rug is what puppies do. He realized that he could choose to appreciate that Luna was alive, happy and bringing joy to her family. That's what really mattered.

On that day, at that moment, that was the lesson a puppy taught a grown man.

The first specialist thought maybe she would last a year. The second thought maybe a few months, but Luna only could hold on a few weeks.

A few days after going home, Luna died with her family by her side in the vet's office. In the end, she could barely lift her head, but she knew her family was there. She tried to lick David's face one last time before saying goodbye. The entire hospital staff was in tears that day, including the veterinarian.

It was one of the saddest days in David and Gloria's life, but to their amazement, someone had reached out to volunteer their dog to donate a kidney to Luna. It was weeks too late, but what a shock it was for a stranger to put their own dog at risk to keep another one alive. David and Gloria were comforted knowing that good, selfless people do exist.

Because I don't like ending this story on such a somber note, I'll let you know that a few months later, David and Gloria got news they were expecting their first child. David was going to encounter a lot more mischief than a puppy digging in the yard, chewing up shoes, and peeing on the rug. How would David choose to see this whole new level of challenges? That story will be told another day.

So, let dogs be dogs, animals be animals, and kids be kids. Appreciate that they are alive. If they are healthy, appreciate that they are in good health. Appreciate the moments, even if things aren't going according to plan and the behavior isn't what you had hoped.

Law of Fulfillment #2:
The Law of Appreciation

The law of appreciation says that when we count our blessings, we are reinforcing our foundation of fulfillment. There is so much to appreciate and feel grateful for, no matter the circumstances.

That story about the loss of the puppy was a difficult one to write. I had to pause multiple times and walk away as emotions got the better of me. You see, David and Gloria aren't just characters in this story. These are actual events my wife Holly and I experienced in real life. I was David in the story. However sad this experience was, I'm grateful for the experience because it did teach me a very valuable life lesson about appreciating what you have and what we may take for granted. Health, friendships, resources, abilities and opportunities are all gifts that we need to recognize and show appreciation for every day. This is more important than what is on the surface of this law. There is deeper meaning in appreciating what we have that will help set the foundation of fulfillment within ourselves, so pay close attention!

We have choices on how we view things when it comes to challenges we face. We can choose to be angry, frustrated, and vengeful, or we can appreciate what we have and also what we can receive from the experience.

For those of you going through something right now, this law is extremely important to understand and apply. It doesn't matter what you're going through right now and how severe it is; there is someone worse off. What you're going through can be traumatic, even life-threatening, but there is still someone worse off than you. I don't mean to belittle your personal situation, but there are souls who would trade places with you in a heartbeat. Don't believe me? I can prove it. Let's begin here by repeating these words: "I am alive!"

You are alive when others are wishing they were still alive. You woke up this morning when someone else didn't. Even if you are battling major illness, you are alive now to fight another day. If you are battling sadness and grief, you are alive to continue moving forward. If you are battling other traumatic events such as a breakup, an unhealthy marriage, or physical disasters, you are alive and have the power to move yourself forward in life.

We started with counting the blessing that you are alive. Next, let's add your health. This can be a tricky one to appreciate, because a large majority of people reading this book are battling some form of a health condition to various degrees. But you need to see and appreciate that there is a path forward. Appreciate that you live in a day and age where medicine is advancing and diseases are cured or managed now where they were not just a few decades ago. Nowadays, doctors aren't practicing bloodletting, making you drink arsenic, or giving out elixirs with cocaine anymore. Did you know it wasn't common for doctors to even wash their hands until a time well after germs were discovered? That was only about 150 years ago. Doctors used to laugh at the idea of washing their hands before surgery. Now, we are cautioned to not eat a meal without washing our hands.

The point is, if you are struggling with your health, appreciate that there can be a path to wellness whether it be through medicine or good nutrition. If you have your health, then appreciate it because so many others are fighting a threat to theirs.

So, we are up to recognizing two things to show appreciation for: We are alive and we have our health (or at least a path to wellness). Let's keep rolling forward, because there is much more to appreciate.

Do you have your youth? Unless you are the oldest person on this earth, you have youth. Although I would bet the oldest person on earth got there because fulfillment already plays a role in their wellbeing, so they don't need youth. No matter what your age, there is someone older willing to trade those years for your youth. You will never be younger than you are right now, at this very moment. Recognize and appreciate that fact. Has that sunk in yet? OK! Now things are starting to snowball!

Let's look at your family, your friends, and people you count on. Recognize and appreciate they are there. Now, let's add in the resources you may have, such as an income, a home, and your transportation. It doesn't matter what it is or how much it is worth monetarily. There are others desperate to have what you have right now.

Let's look at your opportunities. Don't see any? They are all around you. If you want a better education, if you want to learn a new trade or start a business, or if you just want to know how to play the guitar, opportunities are there for you if you open your eyes. Opportunities often scare people because we fear the unknown and we question the opportunity or our ability to seize it. We paralyze ourselves with questions like "Will it work?" or "Can I even do it?" or "What if it doesn't work?" The questions should be "What if it does work?" and "How will your life be different once you've done it?"

We need to appreciate opportunities, as they are the vehicles to changing our own circumstances. What opportunities would you want to have in front of you right now? Open your eyes! They're there! Appreciate that you live in a world surrounded by so much opportunity that you can unhinge from the familiar and plug into the possible. Let's create a bucket list of what you want to do during your relatively short stint on this planet. Add these goals and dreams and your opportunity to achieve them to your list of things to appreciate.

I hope I got the ball rolling in your head. What other things should you put on your list? How about skills you have? What can you do better than most people you know? Keep growing your list. The length of your list might surprise you. So, if you find yourself wallowing in self-pity, let's sink and destroy those thoughts right now like a neutron torpedo. Do you have days when you feel like you can't win? Dude, snap out of it! You've already won! Just look at your list of the things to appreciate.

> People from a planet without flowers think we must be
> mad with joy to have such things about us.
> – IRIS MURDOCH

When it comes to appreciating what we have, we can get hung up on what we don't have; we tell ourselves excuses for why we can't move forward and improve our situation. One of the many things I learned from Tony Robbins is the difference between resources and resourcefulness. Many people are stuck because they feel they don't have the resources for progress. They say to themselves that they don't have enough money, time, connections, knowledge, or something else. These are resources that we may or may not have. Resourcefulness is the ability to persevere and conquer in spite of a lack of resources.

The astronauts of Apollo 13 didn't make it home from space, after their spacecraft became disabled, because of resources. They came home because of the resourcefulness of the engineers on the ground who devised a solution using boxes, pipes and duct tape so they could breathe in outer space. Apple computers didn't grow from a project in a garage to an industry leader in computers because of resources. It did it on the resourcefulness of Steve Jobs. David didn't bring down Goliath because he had resources such as size, strength or an army tank. He showed courage and was resourceful by figuring out a weakness to exploit in the giant with his slingshot. You get the idea.

Now that you know the difference between resources and resourcefulness, you can see it is more important to have resourcefulness than the resources themselves. The next thing you need to understand is knowing how to be resourceful. The first step is having courage and confidence that you have it in you to figure it out. You may and will probably fail and fall on your face along the way, but perseverance is key. For example, J.K Rowling's first Harry Potter book was rejected 12 times by different publishers. Walt Disney was fired from a newspaper for having a "lack of creativity." Howard Schultz was rejected 242 times before someone invested in his idea that ultimately became Starbucks. There are countless stories like these that illustrate the importance of persistence. Keep moving forward, learning from your mistakes and finding ways to make it work. Be resourceful. Otherwise, you are too focused on what resources you don't have. Focusing on what you have instead of what you don't have is very powerful, and it gives you a level of control and a perspective that is a cornerstone to your fulfillment.

Now that you understand that you need to recognize and appreciate what you have, and that you need to recognize and appreciate that you have the ability to be resourceful in moving down a forward path, let's take this appreciation thing to a whole new level.

The best things in life aren't things at all. Don't consume yourself and define your happiness and fulfillment with money, cars, homes and hot tubs. In the end, do you really want to be the richest man in the cemetery? What really counts is the special moments, the friendships, the fun, and creating memories.

────────────── **Your Mantra** ──────────────

Repeat after me: "Every day, I will count my blessings because there are others desperately trying to be where I am now. No matter my current situation, I always know there is a path forward, and I have the courage and resourcefulness to face and move myself down that path. I will stop and smell the roses and cherish the memories I make along the way."

CHAPTER 5

Law of Preservation

Does the above picture make you nervous? Would you take the time to move the glass to a safer location or would you even bother? If the glass fell, you could have a huge problem on your hands. The carpet would stain, the glass may shatter into a million pieces, and you may cut yourself picking up the pieces. The

Does this picture make you nervous?

cut could get infected, and maybe you'd lose your finger as a result, and then it may even get worse from there.

Maybe you're a laborer, a computer programmer, a surgeon, or some other professional who needs all their fingers. Since you cannot perform your job, you get fired. Wow! That escalated quickly! You are now caught in this downward spiral, all because you didn't move the glass from the edge of the table. It all could have been avoided if you had just moved the glass.

> "It wasn't raining when Noah built the ark."
> – HOWARD HUFF

This simple example is a window into a larger concept. How much effort would you put into identifying and evaluating risks to your happiness and fulfillment? It takes just a moment to move the glass and avoid a cascading catastrophe. What are some wine glasses teetering on the table edge in your life? Should you move them?

A Tale of Two Farmers

Since before I was born, our family raised livestock. Although my dad had experience with cattle, hogs, and horses, all I remember were the sheep that we raised on rented land. The sheep farm was mostly pasture but was surrounded by corn and bean fields. The land was so flat, you could see for 20 miles to the horizon.

Summers were often hot and muggy in this area of southwestern Ohio. The land was not adjacent to any large water sources. Lake Erie was 150 miles north and the Ohio River was 80 miles to the south. The main water source was a tiny creek winding through the flat landscape. Droughts would often strike the area for long periods of time during the long summer months. This would devastate the corn and bean farmers who relied on their harvest to earn a living.

The crop farmers on the sides of our farm would meet at the fence separating their properties and chat every once in a while. One was a corn farmer and the other planted beans. One day, during the early spring, before the crops were planted, the corn farmer used a rented excavator to dig a large hole right where he usually planted some of his crops. His neighbor, the bean farmer, was watching this from the fence and scratched his head. "What in tarnation is he doing?" he said to himself.

The bean farmer hopped the fence and walked up to the heavy equipment as the corn farmer concentrated on the levers and the joystick to guide the digging bucket into the ground to bring up and dump another pile of earth next to the hole. The corn farmer saw his neighbor there looking puzzled, so he shut down the engine so he could hear him talk.

"What on earth are you doing?" the bean farmer asked. "Are you putting in a swimming pool in the middle of your corn field?"

The corn farmer smiled at the joke and simply replied, "Rain is coming."

Puzzled by the short response, the bean farmer shrugged his shoulders and said, "So?"

Not wanting to be rude but knowing time was short as the sun had begun to set, the corn farmer fired the engine back up, smiled at his neighbor and went back to concentrating on his hole. The bean farmer stood there with his mouth open for a second, then he threw his arms up in disgust and walked back towards his side of the fence.

After a week, the bean farmer began to till his field, and out of the corner of his eye, he saw his neighbor with a new piece of heavy equipment digging in another part of his field. The bean farmer hopped off his tractor, and again, he jumped the fence to go and talk to the corn farmer. Again, pressed for time, the corn farmer didn't even bother to shut off his backhoe. He waved to his neighbor but kept on digging.

"What are you doing!?" the bean farmer shouted with his hands around his mouth so his voice projected over the loud engine.

The corn farmer shouted back, "Rain is coming!"

Knowing that every square foot of property was important to contribute to the overall yield of their crops, the bean farmer was stunned he was digging up precious acreage. Annoyed that the corn farmer offered no more explanation, the bean farmer turned back towards his tractor. The corn farmer chuckled slightly as his neighbor stomped off.

Within a few days, the bean farmer finished tilling his fields and he was ready to plant this season's bean crop. The corn farmer tilled his remaining land and was able to plant his corn crop as well.

Spring turned into summer, and boy was it a hot one. There were countless days over 90 degrees and the humidity made it feel like 100 degrees more. Corn is supposed to be knee-high by the 4th of July, as the old saying goes, but the corn farmer's crop was barely at his ankles. The bean farmer's field wasn't fairing any better. The bean farmer kicked up dust along the cracked earth as he walked down his short rows of meager bean plants.

Again, out of the corner of his eye, he saw his neighbor, the corn farmer, with pipes and other supplies. The corn farmer was on his hands and knees laying down pipe and fastening it together. The bean farmer just had to go and inquire one more time. He hopped the fence and walked up to ask his question.

"What is all of this? What are you up to now?" he asked insistently.

Without looking up at his neighbor, the corn farmer simply said, "Rain is coming."

The bean farmer looked up into the bright, cloudless sky. He took off his cap and scratched his head while looking for any rain cloud at all. Frustrated, the bean farmer put his cap back on and shook his arms emphatically as he said, "Rain is coming? Rain is coming?" he repeated. "It hasn't rained for weeks and there is no rain in sight. For weeks, you've been working out here, digging up your precious field, minimizing your crops for this season, and like a lunatic, all you can say is 'Rain is coming'?"

The corn farmer put down his tools for a moment and took off his hat to wipe the sweat off his brow. He looked up at the bean farmer and gave his reply of "Yep."

"Well, you are a darn fool!" the bean farmer scolded. He turned back towards his field to go back. He paused and turned his head back towards the corn farmer as he continued to walk away and said, "Don't come crying to me when you can't pay your bills after you harvest what's left around your holes and ditches."

The corn farmer chuckled and shook his head as he continued to work in the ground.

A few weeks went by and still no rain. Then one day, the bean farmer was working on his tractor in the field when he heard a distant rumble. It had been so long, the sound of thunder was unfamiliar to the farmer. A minute or so later, the sky grew dark and rain started to fall. The rainstorm turned into a deluge and the bean farmer ran into his farmhouse, covering his head from the heavy rain drops. He had a big smile on his face as the rain was a welcome change to a dry field. The heavy rain fell for a while, but just as quickly as it had come, the storm moved on and left the farmers' fields. The bean farmer was pleased to see the rain but it soon all dried up and his field was dry and thirsty again. In fact, the deluge washed out some of his bean crop. The corn farmer didn't fare much better with his field at first. But as more rainless days continued to pass after the sudden storm, the corn next door began to flourish.

The bean farmer was puzzled at the sight of lush green corn coming almost up to his waist. "Why is he so lucky?" the confused bean farmer murmured to himself.

He hopped the fence and walked through the corn rows towards where his neighbor had dug his first big hole. As he walked past the last cornstalks and the field opened up where the hole used to be, a large reservoir of water was revealed to be in its place. Amazed at the sight, the bean farmer looked past the water-filled hole and saw a sophisticated irrigation system taking the place of the ditches the corn farmer dug in the months before. The irrigation system cleverly captured the rainwater and methodically dispersed it throughout the entire field.

Just then, the corn farmer, driving by on his tractor, saw his neighbor and waved. "The rain came!" the corn farmer shouted while waving.

The bean farmer mustered a smile out of his amazement and slowly waved back and softly said to himself, "It sure did."

Now, we got to see all this from afar as we were not crop farmers and raised livestock instead. We saw the bean farmer struggle to barely pay his bills with a mediocre bean crop that season while the corn farmer next door had a bumper crop.

Droughts don't last forever. It's better to make the best of it and prepare for your circumstance to change because…rain is coming.

Law of Fulfillment #3:
The Law of Preservation

The law of preservation says that fulfillment can be preserved if we make an effort to prepare for and avoid an undesirable state. We all have the ability to access and mitigate risks and to manage our stress to safeguard our happiness.

"Be prepared."

– THE BOY SCOUT'S MOTTO

I didn't want to join the Boy Scouts, at least not initially. I was suckered in by a good friend who invited me to a recruiting drive cleverly disguised as a canoe trip. I had a blast on that trip, and then I was invited to a meeting. I went but under protest to my parents. It was then that the troop got a new scoutmaster named Bill whom I connected with. Scoutmaster Bill would unknowingly put me on a path that led me to where I am today, and I'm forever grateful to him. It's funny how we initially resist things that are for our own good. I stuck with the Boy Scouts and learned a lot. I ultimately became an Eagle Scout. I learned that there are no "past" Eagle Scouts. Once you become one, you are always an Eagle Scout. It will be on my obituary. Earning the rank of Eagle Scout opened doors for colleges, scholarships, and many other opportunities. It factored into the college I attended, the job I received after college and then transcended into every opportunity after that.

The Boy Scout motto is "be prepared," meaning that you are always in a state of readiness. I believe this is a great asset for someone, and if you have the mindset of being prepared, you preserve what you have and you are ready to take on new opportunities. What I mean by preserving what you have is that you need to safeguard your happiness and preserve your state of fulfillment. This may be a new way of thinking for you. It's a mindset. For example, I would be extremely unhappy and upset if I were to get a speeding ticket and then have to go to traffic court, pay a huge fine and get points taken off my driver's license. So, to preserve my current state of happiness, I take precautions by not speeding (at least not excessively) and practice defensive driving skills so that some unsafe bonehead driver doesn't have a negative impact on my world.

This is like taking out an insurance policy on your happiness. Why do we buy insurance? Because, it's a small price to pay for peace of mind and to be prepared for replacing our stuff if an undesirable event were to happen. We need to do the same to protect our happiness and state of fulfillment. We need to take out an insurance policy on our well-being. In fact, we need to enact many policies each and every day so we are prepared to prevent undesirable situations.

You probably can identify with more examples, like taking off your shoes in the house so the carpet doesn't get dirty. You may use a coaster under your drink so the table doesn't get water stains. You bring an umbrella along in the event that it will rain. These are small examples, and I am sure you get the idea, but let's ramp this concept up a notch.

You need to safeguard and preserve your happiness by avoiding their enemies. The enemy states of your happiness and well-being are anger, stress, worry, sadness, shame, and fear. You need to know what can lead you to one of these enemy states and do what's reasonable to avoid them. The key is to not be lazy. This requires just a little bit of effort for each, but the payoff can be huge, just like insurance is a small price to pay to help you avoid a real catastrophe.

Let's focus on stress first. There are multiple kinds of stresses in our lives, and each kind can contribute to other feelings such as worry and fear. Stress management is so important for our overall happiness. For you to build a foundation of fulfillment, you will need to practice stress management techniques. The best stress management techniques that give you the best bang for your buck are these:

1. Take Control

Prepare so you can avoid things that can go wrong. This is what we've been talking about in this chapter so far. List the things that make you have anxiety or fear. Prepare by beginning to problem-solve what you can do to mitigate or alleviate your fears of what might go wrong. This is like risk mitigation. What risks are you taking right now, and what steps can you take to mitigate them? Figure that out and do it. It will be worth the effort.

2. Manage Your Time

We only have 24 hours each day, and you need to focus in on the urgent and important tasks. Learn to say "no" to others who are stealing your time for their needs and not contributing to your needs. Signing up for too much is what I call "self-inflicted stress," and reducing or avoiding it altogether will drastically reduce stress levels. Focus only on the priorities and say "no" to everything else competing for your time. Make sure you make time for sleep and relaxation. You can't feel guilty if a low-priority task gets bumped from your to-do list so you can have some "me time."

3. Sleep and Relaxation

These are two separate activities, so do not confuse the two for the same thing. Sleep is sleep. Many of us struggle to get enough sleep, but you need to get in the habit of getting enough for you. Relaxation is uninterrupted "me time." Try meditation. I don't necessarily mean sit on a rug with your legs crossed, your eyes closed, and incense burning as you hum "ommm." Let's make it simple. Set a time for 5-15 minutes, turn off your phone, and sit in a quiet room or in your car and just relax. You may have to tell your significant other or your kids not to bother you during this time. While sitting quietly, don't think about your to-do list. Instead, you can visualize things like your goals in life, and you can reassure yourself you have the abilities to achieve them.

4. Exercise

Physical activity can mitigate stress hormones and restore you to a more relaxed state. The Mayo Clinic calls exercise "meditation in motion." It can help calm your nerves and improve your mood. Regular aerobic exercise improves your metabolism, your health, and your spirit. So, pick something that you enjoy, schedule it into your routine and stick with it.

Next, let's take on worry and fear. I like to group these two together for the purposes of this exercise, because they often overlap. Worry is the fear that something undesirable may happen. I was once told in a training seminar that it is useless and a waste of time to worry. The reasoning is that we can only control what we can control. So, if we are worrying about something we can control, then gosh darn it, do something about it to eliminate your worries! If you don't? Well, then that's just plain lazy, and you open yourself up to accepting the undesirable events. If you are worried about something completely out of your control, then you can see that worrying about it can be a waste of time as it consumes your thoughts.

Shame is an easy one for you to avoid, I hope. Obviously, your moral character has control in avoiding shameful situations. Like Marilyn J. Sorensen once said, "While guilt is the feeling of doing something wrong, shame is the feeling of being something wrong." We may do things from time to time that we regret or feel guilty about, but we are human after all. For those situations, forgiveness is our savior, and whether we need someone's forgiveness or we need to forgive ourselves, those situations can be minimized but not avoided altogether. Shame needs be avoided by adjusting our moral compass, and that takes a little more effort and is probably a whole other book in itself. So, I'm going to assume that you, the reader, have a good heart and don't purposely engage in shameful activities.

The last enemy of happiness that prevents you from building a foundation of fulfillment is sadness. We cannot avoid sadness. Human beings are inherently emotional creatures, and we cannot help but succumb to feelings of sadness in certain situations, such as when a loved one dies, a relationship ends, or we see other people suffering. From time to time, we will experience this emotion, but it should be temporary. Time has a way of dimming our sadness and moving us forward in life. There are those afflicted with chronic depression and sadness, and professional therapy will certainly help. If you are one of those afflicted, then I hope this book lends some hope and comfort as well.

"You cannot prevent the birds of sadness from flying over your head, but you can prevent them from nesting in your hair."

– CHINESE PROVERB

The law of preservation is about safeguarding your future happiness by avoiding events that lead to enemy emotions that will diminish any joy you should feel. Safeguarding your happiness is a form of risk management where you need to make an effort to identify what can go wrong and make an effort to mitigate or minimize the event from happening in the first place. It's like having a balanced financial portfolio where you need to spread out your risk so that a quick downturn doesn't wipe you out.

Your homework from this chapter is to develop a habit of assessing what could go wrong in your life. It could be small mundane things or it could be big undesirable events or a mix of both. Once identified, take action to do what you can to avoid them. Again, it takes effort, but if you're lazy at this, these things will come back to bite you. It's not a matter of if they will happen; it's a matter of when.

─────────────── **Your Mantra** ───────────────

Repeat after me: "I have a duty to assess the enemies of my happiness, and I owe it to myself to take action in mitigating them. I have the abilities to prepare for undesirable events, however unlikely, so that my happiness is safeguarded and cannot be wiped out. I have the ability to manage my stress and to control my time because I deserve a foundation of fulfillment where my happiness can thrive."

CHAPTER 6

Law of a Positive Mindset

"The problem isn't the problem. The problem is your
attitude toward the problem."

– CAPTAIN JACK SPARROW

The Restaurant

My brother and I happened to be in Orlando when Planet Hollywood opened at Walt Disney World. I know, I'm dating myself here, but it was really cool to experience a Planet Hollywood restaurant at the time. Arnold Schwarzenegger, Sylvester Stallone and Bruce Willis came to the opening and were part owners of the franchise. We were there during the prime vacation months, and Disney World and the surrounding areas tend to be very crowded, as you can imagine. With large crowds, came long wait times to be seated at restaurants, especially the brand-new Planet Hollywood.

Upon checking into the restaurant, the host communicated that the wait time would be about 45 minutes, and we sat ourselves at the bar to have a drink and wait. Exactly 45 minutes later, we were called and marshalled to a waiting area while the table was being bussed and prepared. We were seated after a short wait and promptly greeted by our waitress, and we ordered an appetizer. After ordering our meals, my brother and I began a conversation, and about ten minutes later, our meals were brought out but before we even got the appetizer. Within seconds, a manager stopped by to see if everything came out OK, and I informed him about the missing appetizer. He apologized and said he would take care of it right away. One minute later, the manager reappeared with the appetizer and said he was removing it from the bill, which I wasn't asking for or expecting. I thought that was an incredibly generous action on the manager's part. He did not have to do that. The meal was delicious and the service was great, or so I thought. In my mind, my expectations were exceeded and I was delighted. So much so, I wanted to write my gratitude on a comment card, which I did. My brother, who just had the same experience as I did, felt the exact opposite as me. He was furious that I would show appreciation for my experience. I found this fascinating. We both just had the exact same experience but opposing reactions to that same experience. In a situation that delighted me and put me in a good mood, my brother felt upset and it ruined the rest of his night. Why?

A big part of it has to do with expectations. My expectations were that it was the hottest new restaurant in the prime of tourist season, and I expected that I would be waiting and I'd need to be patient with the host, the bartender, and the wait staff for the duration we were there. My brother obviously had different expectations. He was OK waiting for a table but expected to be sat immediately when we were called instead of having to wait a few more minutes while the table was prepared. He expected that the appetizer would come before the meal to the point he would be upset if it didn't. He even had the expectation that I would have the same reaction as him and was upset that I was elated and was writing a comment card recognizing the positive experience I had. He was so upset that I didn't feel the same way, he wrote a comment card admonishing the staff for making his experience unpleasant. A difference in expectations certainly influenced the difference in our reactions to the same event, but I also think there is more to it than that.

Obviously, my perspective of the same set of events was different. My thoughts, which have a more positive outlook, set my expectations for the events. My delightfulness was a result of those thoughts that shaped my perspective. My brother's sense of outrage was a result of his thoughts as well. No one told him he should be angry.

No one involved had plotted to ruin his night, and I for one was hoping my reaction would rub off on him. So, his feelings of irritation and fury were based on choices he had made, not on the decisions of anyone else. But often, people react as if it was someone's goal to ruin their evening, like there was a team of clandestine operatives elaborately scheming for weeks with the sole purpose to make them unhappy. I'm sorry to break it to those who think they have a mortal enemy or two, but you're not important enough to anyone out there to be their sole focus to make your life miserable. To those people who think others are spending all day plotting your demise, I would say you need to understand that others are preoccupied with their own problems. The percentage of people out there who would invest countless hours to make you miserable is extremely small, so don't flatter yourself thinking people are out to get you. Instead, let's spend some time changing our perspective to understand other's points of view. More on that concept later.

One interesting footnote is that my brother submitted his comment card about his "unpleasant" experience and received an apology letter with a coupon for a subsequent visit. I received nothing for my comment card submission, but why should they respond to me? I'm a satisfied and delighted customer. My experience couldn't have been better. Since then, my brother and I have both endured our own journeys of personal growth. He has a much more positive outlook now, and he is currently serving as a minister.

Law of Fulfillment #4:
The Law of a Positive Mindset

The law of a positive mindset is that you will always see the good in things if you view the world with a lens of positivity. Whether what you are seeking is bad or good, you will always view it that way.

Do you feel like a lucky person? You may feel you have your stuff together and things are going OK, or maybe you feel like nothing can go right. Either way, you should really believe that you have won the galactic lottery. No, really, you should. Here's why.

First of all, what a time to be alive! What are the chances that you are alive at the best time in world history? Sure, the world's not perfect, but there has been no other time in human history with as much technology, medicine, knowledge, security and an abundance of opportunity and prosperity.

Secondly, congratulations are in order because you beat out about a million other swimmers during your conception! So, woohoo! Let's high-five! You truly are one in a million!

If that's not enough, let's look at the chances that life even exists on this blue marble we call Earth. It is at the perfect distance from the sun. If Earth were a few miles closer, it would be too hot. A few miles further away, it would be too cold. What are the chances that 14 billion years since the big bang that this molded sphere of iron and rock has the abundance in resources and beauty for you to take part in?

Altogether, this is the equivalent of winning the Powerball Lottery 1,000 times in one day. So, let's recognize and appreciate those facts. If this perspective doesn't contribute to your positive mindset, then you can probably stop reading this book right now. Seriously, if that doesn't do it for you, then you may be beyond my help, and by the way, check your pulse to make sure you are alive.

Knowing that all these things happened in your universe by chance and they were completely outside your control reminds us to show some appreciation for how lucky we are to be alive today.

"We can complain because rose bushes have thorns or
rejoice because thorn bushes have roses."

– ABRAHAM LINCOLN

There are two basic rules that apply when it comes to the outlook of your future:

1. **You will always find what you're looking for** - If you are always looking for the good in things, you will always find it. If you are critical and are looking for the bad, you will find that too.

2. **What you focus on always gets bigger** - If you are focused only on your problems, they will become bigger. If you only focus on what's going right, more things will go in your favor.

These two rules are crucial in your understanding of human behavior and why people are seemingly negative or positive within their daily routine. You may or may not have a positive outlook, but if you do, we often find ourselves in the midst of negative mindsets that can affect our positivity. It can feel frustrating and overwhelm us at times. We all know at least one person in our lives for whom things are never going quite right, or they always seem to find something wrong with everything. I call these type negative outlookers.

When negative outlookers are present, the positive outlookers are often berated with thoughts and opinions that are contrary to theirs, and this creates unwelcome friction and can drive a wedge between family members and friends.

The more positive types of people tend to avoid the negative outlookers and the more critical types at all costs. Positive outlookers usually don't associate too much with negative outlookers and excuse themselves when that person enters the room, but positive outlookers want to help change the lens in which the negatives see the world. We positives think it will make both of our worlds a better place. It is possible for the negative outlookers to change their outlook, but they have to be willing to change. That is half the battle, and it is critical before any transformation to a positive outlook can take place. Many of the more negative outlookers are content in their own misery, and by habit, they are comfortable in viewing the bad side of things. They aren't bad people, they just had a series of bad experiences since an early age that formulated their negative beliefs and habits of offering criticism to anyone within earshot.

My advice is not to run for the hills when Negative Nancy or Dougie Downer enters the room. I find it more interesting to observe and, in a non-confrontational way, insert contrary views when I hear an unfounded negative opinion of someone or something.

Again, the negative outlookers aren't bad people, but they miss out on some of the joys of their experience by focusing on the downside. So, if you have a family member or friend who would qualify as a negative outlooker in your life, here are my tips for helping them.

Tip #1: Understand that they have a backstory

The person may not share that backstory with you, but if the person is a close family member or you grew up with them, you may already have an idea what their backstory is. If you met them later in life, understand that if you walked in that person's shoes, especially when they were young, you would know what may have formulated their thoughts and negative habits. Everyone has internal struggles they are dealing with, and with some people, they become external in the form of negative thoughts.

Tip #2: Identify their good traits

Every person has a good side, and we need to identify their best qualities so we can focus on and build upon them. What do they value? What brings them joy? Who do they look up to? Answers to these questions can lead you to their good qualities. Once you appreciate their good qualities in addition to understanding that there may be internal struggles they are dealing with, you can begin to encourage a more positive view of what's around them.

Tip #3: Take an indirect approach

You need to understand they may not want any help. Remember that anyone who isn't open to change, won't change. They may feel they are perfect in their way of thinking and enjoy being negative and critical. Some feel that is their place in the world, so they may feel they will lose their purpose if they change who they are. We don't want to confront their views head on. We just want to tweak how they think, not change who they are. For someone who isn't open, we need to take an indirect approach and use techniques that make them think about and question their thoughts rather than telling them what they should think. Instead of calling them out, offer an alternative point of view that is more positive and let them stew on it.

Tip #4: Don't fall into the argument trap. You won't win.

The reason you don't want to challenge their thoughts directly is that many negative outlookers may take it as a personal attack and would love to argue with you. In fact, they are often experts in debating. Their negative habits have given themselves years of experience in dealing with contrarians and people challenging their opinions. They have mastered the arts of denial, deflection, blame, and excuses. They will drag you down to their level and beat you with expertise. Take a more subtle approach.

Tip #5: Kill with kindness

Notice the tip doesn't say "kill *them* with kindness." We don't want to kill them. We want to kill, or at least subdue, their negative way of thinking. We can do that by nullifying their negative comment with a positive one. For example, if they say something mean about a particular person, add a comment that humanizes that person and diffuses the negative comment.

Negative Nancy may something like "Did you see Brenda's necklace? What dollar store did she buy that from?"

You may diffuse the negativity by responding with something like. "I don't think it's ugly. Maybe one of her kids bought it for her, and besides, she obviously likes it."

If Dougie Downer says something like, "Oh God, there's Chad. He's really full of himself."

You may respond back with something like, "Yeah, he comes across as confident. I bet it really helps him earn a living with his corporate job."

These examples show how you can counter the negativity without being confrontational and be kind at the same time. And, it doesn't have to just be about people. The same approach can be taken with negative comments or actions towards places and things as well.

Now, if you are the focus of Negative Nancy or Dougie Downer, and they launch a direct personal attack on you, there is always a mature and simple way to diffuse their comment and redirect the focus to something else.

In a scene from the movie *The Big Lebowski*, "the Dude" was confronted with a sharp personal attack in which he calmly responded with, "Well, that's like…just your opinion, man." This is a great and funny example of deescalating a potential confrontation.

The key is to not get defensive and to avoid escalation of the situation to a full-out argument. Alternatively, find out what brought on the personal attack. We can do this by asking questions to the affronting individual. You may ask them, "What's wrong? Did I offend you in some way I'm not aware of?" Or, you may ask, "What's going on? Did something happen that's upsetting you? Can I help?" This technique is redirecting the focus off of you personally and to the deeper issue that has brought out the attack. Now, at this point, they may either want to talk about that issue, or they may get frustrated and cease the personal attack, or they may double-down and amp up their attack on you. If they amp it up, probably the best thing to do is to remove yourself from the situation and let things cool off. If they get frustrated and remove themselves from the situation or if they want to talk about their problems, you were successful in the redirection and can work to resolve the real issue if you choose.

There will be situations and people who are not worth your time and effort to change the lens in which someone views the world. These people aren't people. They are "poople." Why? Because they are the ones who suck the joy right out of the room, and you feel like you're standing there with a big smelly bag of crap. Do not waste any more of your precious time with poople. You're not the jackass whisperer. We sometimes have to weed the garden of people in our lives. Remove the poople from your life. Eliminate the people you don't appreciate, and seek out and replace them with like-minded people, especially those who can help you grow.

These tips and more can be a whole book in itself. The main thing is, if this person adds value in your life, love them where they are, appreciate their good traits while subtly making them aware that there are valid, alternative ways to view the world in a more positive light. And, let them stew on it and struggle with these thoughts so they may transform into a new way of thinking. There are many daily exercises in the last chapter of this book that will help change someone's outlook to be a lot more positive. In fact (shameless plug alert), you can give this book to them as a gift. What's more indirect and subtle than that?

If you disagree with any of this advice, I would simply respond to you with, "Well, that's like...just your opinion, man."

"The lion does not lose sleep over the opinions of sheep."
— ANONYMOUS

There is something liberating about not caring what others think of you. First of all, no one is preoccupied or obsessed over what you are and what you do. I'm sorry to be the bearer of bad news. Even if you are a social media diva, the vast majority of followers are preoccupied with their own lives. So, why preoccupy yourself in winning the approval of anyone else but you? There is absolutely no way to win the approval of everyone you know. Even if you're a carpet and let everyone walk all over you, someone's going to complain that you're not flat enough. If this is you, we've got to talk.

You will never be happy if you spend most of your time pleasing others. You are not here on the earth to be someone else's muse. First, spend some time on what brings you joy that does not involve someone you know. Is it an activity such as sports or games? Maybe something intellectual such as reading or writing. Maybe it's helping less fortunate people. Maybe it's a guilty pleasure such as a T.V. show. Whatever it is, 50% of your free time should be spent on your joyous activities. Make sure you mix and match different activities to fill the 50%.

Second, let's add some people you know. I'll assume you are or have already weeded the garden of people in your life and removed anyone who doesn't contribute to your wellbeing. Let's add the close friends and family we enjoy spending time with and create another 40% of activities. More on the topic of friends and family will come in the next chapter.

Ok. That leaves 10% of time for the rest of the world. This could be people we're obligated to spend time with. Certain family members will fall into this category. This could be building rapport with co-workers outside of work. We are not always obligated to meet with co-workers outside of work, but it may help your career if you get to know or learn to get along with some of them.

If you are a people-pleaser and you feel the frustration, anxiety, and anxiousness that comes with being one, let's take a deep breath and evaluate the state we have put ourselves in. Yes, you put yourself in this position, but it's not all your fault. Others have mastered some skills and placed themselves over you. Skills like passive aggression, manipulation, and subtle bullying can take advantage of your kindness and generosity. Once you recognize that you are a people-pleaser and others may be taking advantage of this, congratulations! This is a difficult but critical first step.

The next step is to look at establishing some boundaries with what is acceptable and tolerable behavior on their part and with how you will react if the lines are crossed. Boundaries are invisible barriers that keep people from coming into our space if their purpose is to abuse your trust.

Some examples of setting boundaries might include removing yourself from their lives, at least temporarily, if they abuse your friendship. Maybe it's calling them out when they say something offensive or demeaning. It might be standing up for yourself after you're disrespected.

Hopefully, you have some ideas on how to take back control of your own joy instead of trying to please others. But, what about society and the pressures they may bring? They can also have an impact, but we have to let go of those feelings and replace them with feelings of our own joys and fulfillment.

Laughter heals a lot of what hurts

We begin to laugh at 3 months of age. Little is known about why we laugh and what mechanism is responsible in our brain, but we do know that laughter is universal across all humans. Laughter is an unconscious response that is difficult to control when we see or hear something funny. We even laugh at laughter itself.

There is a lot of power in laughing. Laughter connects and bonds us with others. It adds levity to our boring lives and even gives us a health boost. It makes perfect sense that laughing is good for us just as much as a positive attitude is good for us. Studies have shown that people who are able to laugh at situations rather than being angry or embarrassed have fewer heart attacks and better blood pressure. Let's say you were at a restaurant and spilled wine on yourself. That's probably something we've all done before. Would you laugh and make light of the situation or would you get upset or be embarrassed at the situation? It's better, at least from a health position, to laugh at those situations. It's just like the Elbert Hubbard joke says, "You shouldn't take life too seriously. You will never get out of it alive."

If you have a positive mindset, you will see the humor in things. Being able to laugh at yourself is a sign of self-confidence and security. Our primal ancestors laughed to communicate that all was well and everyone should relax. Laughing at yourself communicates your self-assurance, which is disarming and attractive to others. Would you rather be around someone who laughs when they spill something on themselves or someone who gets angry and throws a fit? You'd probably feel uncomfortable and would find a reason to remove yourself from the room if someone threw a fit. If someone laughed, you may laugh along with them and bond more in a meaningful relationship. So, my suggestion to you would be to see the humor in the situation, make jokes, and laugh at yourself. That's how bonds are formed and memories are created.

Life is too short to be serious all the time. So, if you
can't laugh at yourself, call me...I'll laugh at you.

- ANONYMOUS

———————————— **Your Mantra** ————————————

Repeat after me. "I have a choice when it comes to how I view
the world. Whatever view I choose is what will become, and
whatever I focus on will get bigger. I choose to view the world
through a lens of hope and brightness. I choose to focus on what
went right or may go right instead of what went wrong or may
go wrong. I have the power to release myself from the prison of
what others think and to enjoy the freedom of my own thoughts
and desires."

A funny story on having a positive mindset

My college friend, whom we called John, has an
interesting story about his first days at school. He is
from Europe and his name is pronounced more like
the name Juan but it is spelled J-O-A-N. We called him
John because in America, Joan is predominately a girl's
name. So, you can imagine the honest mistake a housing
administrator made by placing Joan in the all-girls dorm
at college. You can also imagine Joan's delight as he was
an 18-year-old boy living in an all-girls dorm.

The mistake was not caught immediately, and Joan
wanted to milk this opportunity as long as he could.

He got away with it for some time because each student had their own room and bathroom. Now, you may be thinking that you had to share a room or a bathroom with others in college, but we went to a very expensive school where some had the luxury of not having to share. Joan had long hair and a feminine build, so he was able to carry on the ruse even though he made for an unattractive female by most standards. At least, unattractive to some.

You see, the security company hired a part-time guard named Fred to man the front door to the girl's dorm. The school was adjacent to a bad part of Cleveland, and security was a good deterrent to crime. Fred was a young guy in his twenties, and he was always polite and smiled at everyone who was going in or leaving the dorm. Fred was sweet on Joan and thought she looked like no other girl at school. Knowing what you now know about Joan would explain that. But Joan's European accent, although in a deeper voice, cast a spell on Fred, and he was smitten with "her."

Fred began to show his affection towards Joan by asking about her interests and making small talk every time she came or went. Fred didn't beat around the bush. He was very direct and asked Joan out on almost every occasion. Joan always acted flattered but rebuffed his advances. Undeterred, Fred persisted in his pursuits, and Joan became more and more frustrated by the unwelcome advances but wanted to keep his secret intact for as long as possible.

Things came to a head one day when Fred amped up his game and spoke to Joan about his vision for them together and living happily ever after. Joan saw an opportunity to be direct with Fred and let him down so that his pursuit of "her" would end.

"Look Fred, you're a nice guy and I admire your persistence, but it just wouldn't work out with us," Joan said. "I'm from Europe, and I'll go back there someday, so I just don't see it working."

"That's OK," Fred responded. "I've always wanted to live in Europe!"

The conversation was not going in the direction that Joan had hoped. Joan was shooting from the hip here and thought of another idea.

"Fred, I would make a terrible partner for you. I don't even like to cook," Joan said with a frown.

"That's OK. I like to eat out anyway," Fred said happily.

"But Fred, I'm messy and don't like to clean." Joan was starting to grasp at straws here.

"That's OK. Neither do I, and we can hire a maid," Fred said with a smile.

Joan was extremely frustrated at this point. Nothing he said was discouraging Fred's advances. Joan was exhausted with the conversation, and knowing that the jig would be up sooner or later, Joan decided to let Fred down once and for all. Joan took a step back and took a deep breath.

"Well, Fred," Joan said before taking another deep breath. "The reason I won't go out with you is…." Joan unfastened his belt and lowered his jeans to his knees and in a deep manly voice said, "…I'm a man!"

Fred's expression didn't change at all. He simply looked down at Joan then looked back up at his face, smiled and said, "That's OK. Nobody's perfect!"

CHAPTER 7

Law of Personal Connection

"If you're always trying to be normal, you will never know how amazing you can be."

– Maya Angelou

Law of Fulfillment #5:
The Law of Personal Connection

The law of personal connection is that fulfillment is maximized when we personally connect with others. Our DNA is hardwired with the need to connect with others in a meaningful way.

In this chapter, I'm going to rapid-fire a lot at you about personal connection because there are so many facets that are so powerful to understand for you to solidify your fulfillment in bedrock and to become bazooka-proof in life. We really are talking about true superpowers that you may not know you have. Through human connection, you have the power to control the weather for those who are closest to you. Are you setting your days (and theirs) to sunny or are there storms coming? You can ruin someone's day or make someone's day. It's just a choice you make. After this chapter, you may never look at human connection and human interaction the same way again.

The need for us to connect with others is hard-wired into our DNA. It starts with our family. We do not choose our family but we immediately connect with our parents and then siblings if there are any. I am the youngest of five kids. I was what you call an "oops baby." There is eight years separating me and the next youngest, so I got to experience what it was like growing up with a large family and also what it was like being an only child after all my siblings left home.

Maybe you had siblings or maybe you were an only child. When it comes to people's families, it can be a mixed bag. Some were born into loving homes while others had challenges and struggles with their family life. Many have strong, unbreakable bonds with family while others may have written off the family they were born into. That's why it's important to group our close personal friends into this section as well. You may not get along with the family you were born into, but you may have created strong bonds with a family that you made. Either way, personal connection is crucial for your foundation of fulfillment.

> "In the Practice of Tolerance,
> one's enemy is the best teacher."
> -DALAI LAMA

Two Powerful Superhero Skills: Acceptance and Tolerance

At least in recent history, there has never been more polarization in American politics. I see people from every side getting worked up and bent out of shape over any political issue. Civility has taken a backseat to pointed opinions, which often stoop into personal attacks. It's a sad situation that seems to be getting worse instead of better. There is a general and fundamental lack in tolerance and acceptance of other points of view. This fundamental deficiency within the general public is undermining people's abilities to feel fundamentally fulfilled and to experience the joy of diversity and alternative views. Instead, we tend to get angry and extremely upset if someone's opinion is different from our own, and we tend to attack them personally for even considering a different viewpoint. We need to recognize that intolerance of differing views is unhealthy for us personally and as a society. Being closed-minded caps your growth as a human being.

There are two fundamental truths that one must recognize about diverse thoughts. One is that there are other valid points of view, and the other is that it's OK for others to be wrong.

Have you ever been wrong about something that you thought was right? If so, isn't there a possibility that a belief you have right now might also be wrong? The problem is, you have no idea what that might be, so wouldn't it be appropriate to have an open mind on any topics and consider a different way of thinking? Too me, that's not only necessary to grow yourself but it is a huge sign of intelligence to have the capability to learn new thoughts and replace false beliefs with ones that are true.

So, open your mind to all points of view for consideration. Yours may not be as true as you thought, and there may be better thoughts out there, but if your mind is closed, you just capped your ability to learn and understand.

If you are open-minded and consider alternative views, you may also validate your beliefs to be true. When this is the case, it is not necessary to berate others who believe differently. It's OK for them to be wrong. Maybe they are the one who is not open to other ways of thinking, and they are the ones limiting their personal growth. It's OK for them to be wrong. Just accept that they have their opinion, which differs from yours, and respect their dignity as a human being. They are not an enemy. Closed-mindedness and intolerance are the enemies.

Acceptance and tolerance are superhero skills that are way too scarce in today's society. Be the superhero and practice these skills at every opportunity. You may be surprised by the respect you'll get from others when you show consideration and respect for their points of view.

> "To forgive is to set a prisoner free and discover
> that the prisoner was you."
> **–LEWIS B. SMEDES**

The Liberating Power of Forgiveness

Just like most small towns, there isn't much to do when you are young and still growing up. When I was in third grade, one of my favorite activities was fishing. There was a small creek close to where we lived, and a certain spot was especially good for fishing. It was a secluded fishing hole surrounded by trees, but the fish always seemed to bite, so it was one of my favorite spots.

The town I grew up in was small and the income level for most families was pretty modest. Even though our family's income was pretty small, we considered ourselves middle-class for our community. Many of the kids from school came from families below the poverty line. One particular classmate named Travis came from one of these families. They rented one side of a duplex that was extremely modest. Travis was on the bigger side of most of the kids and loved to play rough at recess and tease the girls, and he acted tough around the boys.

I was on the bigger side for my size at that young age. I liked to play catcher for my Little League teams, and I loved to play football. I was not a fighter. All through grade school, I was able to avoid confrontation and tried to deescalate confrontational situations that either myself or my friends were involved in. School yard fights were uncommon but occasionally happened. Travis was usually involved. I got along with Travis for the most part, but I kept my distance. At some point, he felt compelled to befriend me, or so it seemed. He and I would go fishing with some of our mutual friends. We acted tough, and even though we were boys, we saw ourselves as men and talked about things that made us look tough and grown up. This is the era of Arnold Schwarzenegger and Sylvester Stallone movies. We watched these films through idolizing eyes, and we saw their characters as our alter egos. Travis and I became friends.

One day, while walking home from school with Travis and others, Travis said to me that he wanted to fight me. I brushed it off and scoffed at the idea. Travis and I continued to fish together, but he often bullied other kids and exhibited his bravado for all to see. I knew Travis came from a poor family, and even at that young age, I realized that it was important to him to feel big and important around his schoolmates. On another walk home, Travis again said he wanted to fight me. Again, I brushed him off and continued walking. I knew what he was thinking. He could elevate his status in the school yard by beating up a "bigger" kid. I was not a fighter, and the conversation just made me uncomfortable.

On a walk home one day, Travis jumped out and punched me right in the chest as hard as he could. It hurt like hell, but I didn't want to show it. I just spun around and walked away like nothing even happened. This frustrated Travis, my so-called friend.

On a warm spring day, Travis and a few of his friends went fishing with me to my favorite fishing spot. We began talking about whatever 9-year-old boys talk about when they get together as we put worms on our hooks and cast the bait into the water. I was intently watching my bobber on the surface of the water as Travis walked up, grabbed my favorite fishing rod out of my hands and threw it into the deep water. Just then, a couple of his friends came up behind me and grabbed my arms. Travis got in my face and said, "Do you remember I said that I wanted to fight you someday? Well, that day is today." Just as he finished his statement, he hit me square in the jaw as hard as he could. I remembered the stinging pain in my face as it happened. He delivered a few more blows to my head and body as his friends let me go in anticipation of me fighting him back. Instead of fighting him back, I sunk down on my butt and sat with shock and confusion. I didn't know what to do or think. My so-called friend, whom I enjoyed to fish with, along with my other schoolmates, had just attacked me. Between the thoughts of betrayal and the thought of my favorite fishing rod sitting at the bottom of the creek, I sat there stunned. Travis seemed frustrated that I wasn't fighting him back. His frustration turned to the satisfaction of his sucker punches landing on my face, and he and his friends left as I sat there in the middle of the woods in shock. After the stun wore off, I sat up and began to walk home. I remember crying most of the way home, although I tried hard to hide my tears.

Upon arriving home, I was embarrassed to tell my parents what had actually happened. I was bruised on my cheek and bawling like a baby. I concocted a story about tripping and falling on some logs as my fishing pole fell into the creek. My dad walked me back to the fishing hole and was able to hook the rod with a long tree branch and bring it back to the surface. That made me feel a little better, but I was struggling with the betrayal of my friends and the embarrassment of getting sucker-punched by a bully. What would the kids think as they learned of my defeat? Would Travis brag of this at school the next day? I was feeling like a victim, wondering if I could have handled the situation differently. I felt ashamed for feeling scared to fight him back.

The next few days, I endured the teasing from schoolmates as Travis basked in his glory of beating me up. After a while, the teasing stopped, and the schoolmates forgot and moved on and so did Travis, who was now focused on his next victim. We never walked home from school or even spoke again. The feelings of shame, betrayal, and sadness did not leave me easily. I began to question friendships as I learned a lesson that some only pretend to be your friends but have hidden motives.

As time went on, I chose friends carefully and had my guard up through the rest of grade school and in middle school and through most of high school. The embarrassing event shaped how I would trust people for years to come. A few years later, I happened to ride past Travis's house. He lived in one of the poorest sections of town, in a duplex made of cinder block with windows that had no screens. He was shirtless, sitting out front with his siblings and neighborhood kids. I noticed the conditions in which he had to live every day. They had next to nothing, and I felt pity as our family, living in a humble household, had so much more. At this time, I forgave his actions even though he never asked for it. I realized I needed to forgive him for me to get past the toll it had taken on me emotionally.

Several years later, when I was seventeen or eighteen, I ran into Travis at a community meeting. There were several dozen people there, but there was a small enough number that he saw me and I saw him. Upon seeing each other, neither one of us spoke. I stared at him briefly, and then he sheepishly lowered his head and looked in a different direction. I sensed he was ashamed of being such a bully to me and others almost a decade earlier. I wasn't sure if that was truly his feeling, but that helped me complete the process of forgiving him for my own healing.

"Forgiveness doesn't mean you excuse the crime. It just means you're no longer willing to be the victim."

– UNKNOWN

There are many facets to forgiveness that you will want to understand. There are those who need our forgiveness and there are those whom we need to forgive. There is a difference. A person may have wronged us in some way and has recognized it and wishes to be forgiven.

Then there are those who may have wronged us but have not recognized it or don't even care. We need to forgive them so we may move on. This one is most common but is also the hardest to do. There is great strength in recognizing that we need to forgive those who are not asking for it. Not so much for them, but for ourselves.

I came across an obscure study done in the Netherlands by researchers at Erasmus University. They had their human subjects write about a time that they either gave forgiveness or withheld it. They then had the subject perform a physical feat. The ones that wrote about giving forgiveness substantially outperformed the ones that wrote about withholding forgiveness. While not conclusive, it does exemplify how withholding forgiveness can also hold us back physically.

Faults make us human. There is no escape to making mistakes in life, and people will get hurt along the journey. When we hurt one another, we can ask to be forgiven. When we are the ones hurt, we can do the forgiving. Holding a grudge is unhealthy. The perpetrator is usually free in their thoughts and obliviously living life while we stew in anger and are barred from living ours. What good can become of plotting the demise or revenge on those who may not have even realized they wronged us in the first place? What power is bestowed on those who can look past the wrongful deed, empathize with the offender, and forgive them surreptitiously within ourselves? Also, studies have shown that reminding a person of a grudge increases their heart rate and blood pressure. Alternatively, forgiveness is linked to better heart health but only if you truly forgave at an emotional level and not just by going through the motions of forgiving.

Empathy is a skill worth practicing. When someone wrongs you in some way, do you assume they meant to harm you? Even if they did mean to harm you, do you assume it's for malicious reasons? Alternatively, do you step back and consider that you might have wronged them in some way and that this is their way to get even? Or maybe, they are struggling with a flaw that extends their spiteful behavior. I like to think that there is an alternative story to the one that is evident on the surface. I think too much of people to conclude that their deviant behavior is pure evil; something else may have caused this person to intend harm. In other words, understand that the wrongful deed does not define the offender.

Once you understand that you have the ability to change your mindset so you're not focused on a single wrongdoing towards you, but you instead see a deeper meaning and broader perspective on what is going on in the offending person's life that may have brought on the offensive behavior, you can begin to separate yourself from the conflict and feel less like a victim and more like someone with a strong will. This revelation and way of thinking is a position of empathy or even sympathy for the offender, and it puts you on a path of compassion and forgiveness, even if the offender is not asking for it. Again, forgiveness is more about your mindset and wellbeing than the one who wronged you in the first place.

I believe there are three steps to forgiving someone:

1. Recognize that the offending deed does not define the person.

2. Step back and empathize with the offender and explore alternative reasons for their behavior.

3. Most importantly, understand that forgiving someone is about setting yourself free so you are not imprisoned with feelings of animosity and hate.

How to ask for forgiveness

Alternatively, if you are the one in the wrong and want someone's forgiveness, there is a right way to ask for it and a wrong way. The wrong way is to justify your actions and explain your intent. If you take this approach, the other person may feel that the two of you are being pulled into a confrontational exchange of excuses instead of recognizing how they have been affected by the act itself.

The best way to ask for forgiveness is to acknowledge how your actions impacted the other person. It shows respect for their feelings and their perspective. It puts you both on the same page. The other person will feel that you truly understand their viewpoint, that you are showing consideration for how they feel and that you are genuinely sorry for your actions.

How many husbands out there have ever forgotten their anniversary or maybe their wife's birthday? Hasn't happened to me (yet), but I haven't been married all that long so there may come a day. Hopefully, for my sake, that day never comes. But if a husband forgets their anniversary, feels regret, and asks for his wife's forgiveness, how do you think his wife will feel if he starts off by giving her reasons and excuses as to why he forgot and states that his intention was not to make her upset? What if he says that his job is stressful, and that he has a big meeting tomorrow, or that he has a lot to do and simply forgot? Do you think she will feel empathy, or do you think that she may feel even angrier because the husband is seemingly saying it's not his fault? I would bet that she would feel obligated to remind him that he can still remember his bowling league, the date of his golf trip, and when Star Trek convention comes to town but can't remember the date he married her. God forbid this unfortunate event from ever occurring in anyone's marriage, but in this example, the husband would have a better chance at being forgiven if he were to tell his wife that he feels shame for upsetting her and making her feel unappreciated, or making her think that he doesn't see their marriage as important when in fact he does. If he recognizes her feelings and how his forgetfulness has made her feel and if he shows genuine remorse, he might have a better chance of forgiveness and being married a little longer so he can make up for it on their next wedding anniversary.

"It's not about what we have but who we have."
- WINNIE THE POOH

The superpower with the biggest payoff

A father and young son left the downtown movie theater after watching the latest superhero thriller on the big screen. The little boy was beaming after seeing a team of superheroes defeat the super-powered antagonists to make everything right in the world, at least until the next ill-willed villain visits the city. The boy was thinking and daydreaming of a world with superheroes walking among us, sometimes in disguise, waiting for the next wrong to be righted. His wondering imagination made him curious.

"Dad?" the young boy asked.

"Yes son?" the father replied.

Pausing for a second, the boy asked, "Do you know anyone with superpowers?"

Without hesitation, the father replied, "Yes, I do."

"You do?!" the surprised boy shouted.

"Of course," the father said. "I have a superpower, and so do you."

The boy was surprised by his father's answer and was excited. "Really?! What is it?"

The father paused for a second to think. He put his finger to his cheek and thought of an idea and said, "Let me demonstrate it for you."

The father and son walked up to cross the street but the light was green and there was an older woman standing at the crosswalk waiting for the light to change. She had a stoic look with a slight frown and was wearing a bright blue hat. The boy and his father walked up to wait beside the woman. The father saw his chance.

"That is a lovely hat you are wearing," the dad said to the woman.

The woman looked at the dad with wide eyes and her mouth slightly open as she was surprised. She looked down at the boy and then back up at the dad and said, "Why thank you! I love this hat. It was given to me many years ago by my late husband, and it reminds me of him whenever I wear it."

The father then said, "Well, I can tell he had great taste in hats, and he obviously was thinking how great you would look when he bought it for you."

The traffic light turned and the three began to cross the street. Before parting ways, the old woman said, "Thank you so much for saying that; you two have really made my day!" The women turned the other way and began to walk. The dad and his son both noticed that the woman's demeanor was much different than before. The boy noticed she was now smiling as she walked, her gate was a little livelier and her head was held slightly higher than when they first walked up to her.

The father and son stood still as they watched the women walk away. "You see, son?" the father said. "We just helped brighten the day of an old woman."

The son, still a little puzzled by the experience, said, "But Dad, all you did was compliment that old hat she was wearing."

"Yep," said the dad.

The boy continued his puzzled thoughts. "Now she looks so different than when we first saw her. She's happy now."

His father explained, "It doesn't take much to be kind to others and to change their world, even if it's for just a day. That is why it is a superpower that both you and I have." His young son looked as his father in amazement and began to nod slowly as his father's words sank in. "Are you ready to try it?" asked the dad.

The two began to continue their walk home when they passed the city hospital. The entrance was buzzing with activity as hospital staff and patients were going in and out of the doorway. As they continued walking down the sidewalk, the boy caught a glimpse of an older man who looked a little down. He stood next to the hospital wall with a blank face, staring at the ground. The boy noticed a white band around his wrist, and after just witnessing his father's demonstration with the old woman, the boy got an idea and saw his chance.

What the boy did not know was that the man he was approaching had stage-four cancer and was undergoing an experimental treatment after chemotherapy had failed. The man had lost hope and was contemplating quitting the experimental trials held at the hospital, as he wasn't seeing much progress.

The boy let go of his father's hand and went up to the man, who nervously looked up as the boy approached.

"I like your wristband," said the boy.

The man mustered a small smile and grabbed his wrist to move the white hospital band back and forth. "You mean this?" the man asked. The boy nodded slowly, looking up at the man. The boy's dad stood a few feet away and watched. The man knelt down to the boy's level and said, "Well, thank you, but this band means that I'm a patient here, and that's not a good thing."

"But, why?" the curious boy asked.

The man, realizing that he just engaged with the curiosity of a child, smiled and said, "Well, it means that you are sick and need to get better."

"Are you getting better?" the boy asked back. His dad was now nervous that his young son's curiosity was getting a little too personal with the stranger.

The man nervously chuckled, looked at his feet and then looked back at the boy. "Well, not yet, but healing can be a slow process."

The boy's curiosity was replaced with confidence. It was evident in his voice when he said with conviction, "I know you'll get better."

"Oh, yeah?" said the stranger. "You think so?"

"Sure I do!" said the boy. "Just look at those other people." The boy pointed to the front door where staff were pushing wheelchairs and gurneys with patients in and out of the hospital and in and out of ambulances. "I don't know about them, but you are standing here without needing anyone's help. They are so sick that they need to be pushed around by someone else."

The stranger quickly reflected on the simple, naïve thoughts the boy has just stated. The young boy could not see the sickness on the inside of the stranger's body. The stranger clinched his lips together and nodded in agreement with his new young friend. "You know what? You're right. I'm not in that bad of shape. Thank you for putting that in perspective for me."

The stranger stood up and the boy's dad stepped forward smiling at the man and said, "Come on, son. We better be getting home to your mother."

"What is your name, son?" the stranger asked the little boy before leaving.

"Robert," replied the boy.

"My name is Greg," said the man. "It was a pleasure speaking with you, Robert. Thank you for the compliment and for your insight."

"You're welcome!" shouted the boy as he grabbed his father's hand and started to walk away, turning his head back once with a smile. The stranger smiled back and lifted his hat to scratch his head. He was tickled by the sudden encounter with the young boy. Although simple and naïve, the thoughts of the young boy did put his self-pity and wallowing in a different perspective, and he decided to head up to the oncology ward for his treatment.

On the rest of their walk home, the boy pondered the exchange he had with the stranger, as it had not gone the way he anticipated. He expected it to be similar to the exchange between his father and the old woman. The boy was not sure he made the man any happier by giving him a simple compliment.

His father was proud of his son and appreciated the candidness of his words to the stranger. "Son, I bet you did a better job than I did."

"Really, Dad?"

"Yep. Something tells me that man needed some hope, and I think you gave him some hope, which is better than just bettering someone's day."

The boy gleamed with a smile the rest of the way home. Once they were home, the dad put a superhero cape made from a bath towel onto Robert, and the young boy ran around the house giving anyone and everyone compliments the rest of the evening. Mom got several compliments, as did the dog, the goldfish and even the potted plants.

"What has gotten into him?" a pleased but puzzled mother asked the dad.

"Our son is beginning to understand he has a superpower to change the world by changing the world for one person at a time."

The mother, still a little puzzled, since she was not part of the life lesson and the experiences of the day, nodded and said, "Alright. I definitely like his new-found attitude."

Robert soon forgot about his encounter with Greg, the stranger, but the lesson stuck with Robert as he grew up and would seek to practice his superpower almost every chance he got.

He and his father would never see Greg again, and what they didn't know is that Greg continued his treatments and his cancer improved. Although he was never cured, Greg healed to the point his cancer was manageable and lived the rest of his life in a normal fashion. Greg never forgot the encounter with a young little boy named Robert. The exchange between the two, however brief, gave Greg the nudge he needed at the right moment to keep him moving forward with new-found hope. We may never know what the payoff of a little act of kindness, such as a little compliment, might bring.

* * *

I've saved this superpower for last. I find this internal superpower that we all possess to be the most rewarding of them all, and it costs nothing but a small effort. It is the power to make someone else happy, even for just a moment. At the very least, you can make someone's day with the smallest of effort. At the very most, you can change the course of someone's life with only some simple encouragement. When we can connect with someone, even a stranger for the briefest of moments, you can change their world for the better. As the saying goes, you may not be able to change the world, but you can change the world for one person.

Have you ever received a small compliment from a stranger? How did it make you feel? When we get a small but kind compliment from someone, it transforms us, sometimes briefly, into a state of happiness and confidence. We have a little more pep in our step. We find ourselves smiling more. We find ourselves in a good mood. But what's even more amazing is that we tend to pay it forward. Our mood can be infectious to others. We tend to be kinder and pass on a compliment of our own to another. Then another, and so on. Pretty soon, our neighborhood, our office, or the entire shopping mall is beaming with positivity, and it all started with someone paying a kind compliment to you. That is so powerful! Little acts of kindness have a big payoff.

If it's so simple and costs nothing but a moment of our time, why doesn't this happen more often? I would challenge you to answer that question for yourself. When was the last time you gave a small compliment to a complete stranger? What about saying something nice to a friend or family member? Too often, we are so consumed with our own lives, our daily routines, and our own problems that we forget we have the ability to change all of that, even in other people that we interact with on a daily basis. So, the next time you are in a store, say something nice and compliment the clerk or cashier. The next time you eat out, tell the wait staff what a great job they are doing. The next time you are standing in line, compliment the person next you on their hair or what they are wearing. Thank people for the little things that others do for you. Connect with others in small ways that express the very traits that make us good people. These little acts of kindness will have a huge payoff in that you are making someone's day brighter and in turn, it will make you feel like a better human being for doing so.

You see, the abilities to show acceptance, tolerance, forgiveness and kindness are the superpowers of your human soul. Criticism, jealousy, judgement, and indifference are your kryptonite.

Your Mantra

Repeat after me. "My abilities to accept, tolerate, and forgive others are my superpowers. I possess the abilities to change my world and the world for other people, even if it's for only a few minutes, a day, or even a lifetime. Kindness is infectious, costs nothing and the payoff can be immeasurable."

CHAPTER 8

Applying the Laws of Fulfillment to Your Life

"Knowledge has no value except that which can be
gained from its application toward some worthy end."

– NAPOLEON HILL

Now that we have covered the laws of fulfillment, let's apply them to the everyday activities of your life. There is some low-hanging fruit and some simple concepts to implement immediately. With some of the laws, it will take some practice and some getting used to. I've organized this chapter so you get the best bang for your buck by applying these steps in the order they appear.

But first, let's review each of the five laws:

Law of Fulfillment #1:
The Law of Self-Actualization

The law of self-actualization says that you and only you get to decide how you feel at any moment in time. No one has the power to make you feel a way that you do not choose. If you don't make a choice on how you feel, someone else will.

Law of Fulfillment #2:
The Law of Appreciation

The law of appreciation says that when we count our blessings, we are reinforcing our foundation of fulfillment. There is so much to appreciate and feel grateful for, no matter the circumstances.

Law of Fulfillment #3:
The Law of Preservation

The law of preservation says that fulfillment can be preserved if we make an effort to prepare for and avoid an undesirable state. We all have the ability to access and mitigate risks and to manage our stress to safeguard our happiness.

Law of Fulfillment #4:
The Law of a Positive Mindset

The law of a positive mindset is that we will always see the good in things if we view the world with a lens of positivity. Whether what we are seeking is bad or good, we will always view it that way.

Law of Fulfillment #5:
The Law of Personal Connection

The law of personal connection is that fulfillment is maximized when we personally connect with others. Our DNA is hardwired with the need to connect with others in a meaningful way.

Imagine a person who exhibits all the traits we talked about in this book. Now imagine if that person was you. Life is a journey of personal growth, and if you aren't growing, you're dying. Let's start with some simple daily routines that don't take a lot of time and will have a big impact each and every day.

1. Begin and end each day with three things you are grateful for and say "Thanks."

As you begin your morning routine, whether it be while you are showering, brushing your teeth or drinking your coffee, remind yourself of three things that you have and appreciate. It can be a person, a skill, or something material. This will help set a positive tone for the day. When you remind yourself you have a foundation of fulfillment with a pillar of gratitude, fewer things can upset your mood. Remember, if you feel like you are having a moment where you can't win, remind yourself that you've already won.

As you lay down in bed each night, before you fall asleep, remind yourself of the three things you are grateful for and also one thing you are looking forward to in the next day. Doing this will help ease your busy mind, give you a moment of peace, and prepare your brain to see the good things happening tomorrow.

Some people like to journal their gratitude, and that is a great idea. For starters, I would encourage you to just spend a few minutes at the beginning and end of each day thinking of what you are grateful for. For each thing you are grateful for, ask who is responsible for giving you that gift and go thank that person. Maybe it's your parents, a teacher, a boss, or God. Whoever it is, express your gratitude and go thank them.

2. Each day, celebrate a win.

Every day alive is a win. We need to celebrate the little things and the big things. Whether it is celebrating that you survived the workday, completed a project at work, or your kid won a Little League game, go and celebrate. Better yet, celebrate someone else's win. When we celebrate with others, it doubles the joy. Celebrate that friend's promotion, their birthday, or the fact that you both finished another day at the office. It doesn't matter the reason, just pick one. There are plenty to choose from and you should be creative. Celebrate a sunny day, the arrival of your online order, or that you just washed your car.

You don't have to make it a big deal with a fancy meal or a night out on the town. Just go have a cocktail, invite someone over for cookies, get yourself a piece of pie, or grab a quick bite with a friend or family member. The expense is unimportant. The main point is to pick something good that happened, reward yourself, and share the moment with someone.

When we celebrate our collective wins, we are training our brain to see the positive. The more we see, the less room there is for the negative things to creep their way in. So, call up that friend, relative or coworker whom you enjoying spending time with and go celebrate something tonight.

3. Connect with someone, daily.

When you show someone you value their company, even for a few minutes, it goes a long way for you and for them. Reconnecting with someone you don't talk to as often can be very meaningful. Getting to know a coworker or a friend of a friend can lead to unexpected things. You may find out that you have something in common. You may learn something that you didn't know before that will help grow you as a person. You may become friends with their friends someday, and those friends may be more meaningful than your current base of friends. Or, you may find out that they were hurting, but you made their day a little bit better.

This can be difficult for some. I'm introverted for the most part, and this was especially difficult for me at first until I did it a few times. I was forced out of my introverted comfort zone; it was a little awkward in the beginning, but practice makes perfect. What makes it easier now is that I look at every person I meet and wonder what mysterious backstory that person has. Each person's backstory is a mystery to solve. I always wonder what their background may be, what exciting things they have done in their life, and what exciting things they want to do, and I want to hear a fascinating story that they may be hiding. I especially like to talk to older generations. What did they see and do before I was even born? "What was it like to be alive back then?" I wonder and ask them. Many older folks have great stories; this inspires me to talk to more people and to hear about their past adventures and about the famous people they have met or were friends with. It not only inspires me to get their stories but it makes me think about the story of my life.

There is a whole world out there that you aren't even aware of, and when we connect with others, we unlock little corners of that world that may bring more meaning to our own lives, both now and later. Use curiosity and ask questions to people you meet. They say there are only six degrees of separation among us all. The mystery of how we are connected can be amazing once we begin to solve it. Connect or reconnect with friends, friends of friends, coworkers, and strangers. Discover the people who influence positivity and make you grow. The investment you make though connection can payoff dividends down the road.

4. Weed your garden.

Identify the "poople" in your life who drag you down. These are the Negative Nancy's, the Dougie Downers, the dream stealers, the moochers, the drama queens, the naysayers, and the others who may squeeze the life right out of you. Don't buy into the crap they are selling; love them from a distance. They deserve less of your time. You owe them nothing, so quit serving a penance or repaying a debt you don't owe.

It is said that you will become the sum of the five people you hang out with the most. I like to say to the kids that I coach, "Show me your friends, and I'll show you your future." Take inventory of the five people you spend the most time with. Are they adding value to your life, or are they holding you back? Do they inspire and encourage you, or are you just their muse? Are they pushing you to grow, or are they blocking the sun?

It can be difficult to remove someone you've spent a lot of time with from your life. They may resist being removed and replaced with someone better. Anticipate guilt trips, personal attacks and defiant behavior. Again, don't buy their crap! You deserve better, and all the negative resistance should be affirmation that you are doing the right thing.

Grow forward and weed the garden of your life. Replace the "poople" with their opposites. Seek out the influencers, the supporters, the cheerleaders, the dreamers, the givers, and the life-lovers. Your vibe is in your tribe, and if your tribe is made up of people who support you and inspire you, your life garden will grow, and you will be a better person as a result.

5. Don't sweat it.

Nothing hardly ever goes according to plan. How we see it happening in our mind is far different from reality, so expect and embrace change. Constantly set and reset your expectations with each change and stay focused on the good that comes along the way. Take inventory of the things that worry you most. If there is something that worries you, ask yourself if there is something that can be done about it. If not, it's outside your control. If there is something you can do, then decide to do it or take the risk, but be confident and comfortable in your decisions.

Stress is an antagonist to your happiness. By preparing for the worst and hoping for the best, you become more resilient when things go wrong. Manage your stress by taking control of your life. If you don't take control of your life, someone or something else will. Practice good time management by prioritizing activities that bring you joy or an investment in your future. Minimize or eliminate anything else.

6. Work on the new version you.

Personal growth should be a never-ending journey. The human brain craves to learn new things. It is in our DNA to better ourselves. If you're not growing, you're dying, so work on you. Read books, take classes, spend time with a mentor, try new things and go to new places. Get out of your comfort zone and expand your horizons. Take an art class, write a story, or maybe learn to cook. You have an amazing ability to find out what you don't know and then be a master at what you find.

It's not about the goal you reach, but it's about the person you become along the way. Be a better version of you and keep upgrading. The future version of you is waiting for you along the way, but if you don't grow, the two of you will never meet.

Do not compare yourself to others. It's your journey to make, and everyone's journey is different. The challenge, to anyone, is to let go of who you are so you can become the person you should be.

7. Help yourself by helping others

Nothing can replicate the feelings you have when you are able to help someone else. Your foundation of fulfillment can be fortified by changing the world for just one person, if not for many. Look for opportunities to help others. Give your time to causes that are meaningful for you: kids needing a mentor, families that are hungry, animals that need rescued, or even friends who need your support. Every minute and every dollar you give gets repaid tenfold.

You shouldn't try to make everyone happy. That never works out, but become laser-focused with one or two causes that are meaningful to you and see what that will do for your foundation of fulfillment. You don't want to die being the richest man or woman in the cemetery. You can't take it with you, so plan out your estate so at least a portion of it goes to help those in need so your legacy lives longer than you will on this earth.

CONCLUSION

The underlying principle in this book is, you need to create a foundation of fulfillment so your happiness can thrive. Your foundation of fulfillment can be rock solid so your wellbeing is not only resilient, but it is bazooka-proof. Having a consistent feeling of gratitude and confidence is an asset. It sets the stage for consistent mental toughness. The five laws of fulfillment help you understand how to create that foundation, and once it's solid, you will reveal more of the positive and happy things this life has to offer.

You and only you control your thoughts and your feelings. Choosing what you are thinking or feeling at any moment in time is truly a superpower that everyone has, but few understand this power or practice their choice. Dumb and numb people somehow feel entitled to happiness and are looking for someone to blame. They should be looking in the mirror and take off their foggy glasses so they can see that there is an abundant amount of things to appreciate. There are so many things to appreciate, you should lose count.

Good habits include taking steps to protect your peace of mind. Just like insurance protects our houses and cars, put forth effort in avoiding the enemies of your happiness. As discussed earlier in the book, move the glass from the edge of the table and avoid a potential catastrophe. Your fulfillment is an asset and you need to insure it just like any other important asset. Instead of paying an insurance premium, payment comes in the form of small, daily habits of recognizing and avoiding any pitfalls that will impact your state of happiness. These habits will become second nature to you over time.

When you adjust the lens in which you view the world, all the positive things that were always there begin to reveal themselves. When you look for the good, it appears in a big way. If you keep focused on the positive, the good things grow and get better. Laugh at yourself and all the funny things that bond us together. Your confidence and self-esteem will bask in the voice of your laughter.

Your personal growth is weighted by people who don't have your best interests at heart. Likewise, having people who support and inspire you is like tying propellers to your arms so you can thrust forward towards a better version of yourself. Accept others as who they are and don't judge a person unless you want to walk a mile in their shoes. Everyone has a background story different than your own; appreciate the assortment of ideas. When you create connections with others, a synergy is formed and you benefit in the value of the relationships and bonds that are formed. It is inherent in our DNA to help each other and to point out what makes life interesting.

Your attitude will become infectious to others, creating a microcosm of positive people in your corner of the word. Imagine if most people made the same effort. Think of the ripple effect it could have. Your new-found mindset can inspire and encourage others to do the same, and then it can spread from there. It's like tossing a pebble into a quiet pond and watching the ripples spread out from that spot in all directions.

And then, people will begin to cooperate and work together and people will have a better sense of community. Problems get solved, processes are improved, people are healed and it feels good as things start to be as you would want them to be.

This asset you create, your foundation of fulfillment, is unshakable. It is yours and cannot be taken from you. It is the baseline in which all future progress is measured from. It shields you from the bad and propels you toward the good. It is truly a superpower percolating within us all, waiting to be fortified to make you bazooka-proof. Your foundation of fulfillment empowers you to see more clearly, to attract good people, and to provide the confidence and inspiration to change the world or at least change the world for one person. That person is you. Because, you are worth it.

ABOUT THE AUTHOR

Brian Highfield's story of transformation, from a depressed youth with limited hopes and dreams into a successful business person who is now the happiest person he knows, is a story that can teach others how to live a life of fulfillment. Brian retired from the corporate world at the age of 45 after a successful management career at one of the largest communications firms in the world. He went on to create multi-million dollar businesses in the sports and healthcare arenas, and founded the TheBeardedPhilosopher.com to share ideas and principles on the topics of happiness, health, finances, and personal growth. Brian regularly speaks at seminars with people who want to improve their lives or build their business leadership skills. In addition to helping others, Brian loves to be a stay at home dad to his son, Austin and a husband to his wife, Holly. Brian and his family like to snowbird between Sarasota, Florida and Cleveland, Ohio.

My Invitation to You

CPSIA information can be obtained
at www.ICGtesting.com
Printed in the USA
JSHW032258100720
6611JS00003B/153